WHY
SINGLE PARENTS
MATTER

About the author

Professor Amy Brown is based in the School of Health and Social Care at Swansea University where she leads the research centre 'LIFT' (Lactation, Infant Feeding and Translational Research). With a background in psychology, she became interested in experiences of parenting when pregnant with her first baby.

Three babies and a PhD later she has published over 120 research papers exploring psychological, cultural and societal influences on infant feeding, alongside experiences of perinatal mental health, parenting and health. In 2016 she published her first book *Breastfeeding Uncovered: Who really decides how we feed our babies?*, which was updated in 2021. She has since published a further eight books with Pinter & Martin which have helped support parents and professionals around the world.

WHY
SINGLE PARENTS
MATTER

Amy Brown

pinter & martin

Why Single Parents Matter (Pinter & Martin Why It Matters 26)

First published by Pinter & Martin Ltd 2023

©2023 Amy Brown

Amy Brown has asserted her moral right to be identified as the author of this work in accordance with the Copyright, Designs and Patents Act of 1988.

All rights reserved

ISBN 978-1-78066-655-6

Also available as an ebook

Pinter & Martin Why It Matters ISSN 2056-8657

Series editor: Susan Last
Index: Helen Bilton
Cover Design: Blok Graphic, London
British Library Cataloguing-in-Publication Data

A catalogue record for this book is available from the British Library.

This book is sold subject to the condition that it shall not, by way of trade and otherwise, be lent, resold, hired out, or otherwise circulated without the publisher's prior consent in any form or binding or cover other than that in which it is published and without a similar condition being imposed on the subsequent purchaser.

Set in Minion

Printed and bound in the UK by Clays

This book has been printed on paper that is sourced and harvested from sustainable forests and is FSC accredited.

Pinter & Martin Ltd
Unit 803 Omega Works
4 Roach Road
London E3 2PH

pinterandmartin.com

Contents

Introduction	7

PART I:
HOW DOES IT FEEL TO BE A SINGLE PARENT?

1 The highs and lows of single parenting	17
2 Where did the stereotypes about single parenting come from?	32
3 Is there any evidence that children from single parent families have worse outcomes?	42

PART II:
EXPLORING SOME OF THE CHALLENGES OF SINGLE PARENTING

4 Supporting your child through change	52
5 Co-parenting	62
6 Dealing with finances	82
7 New relationships	98

PART III:
SUPPORTING YOU AS A SINGLE PARENT

8 Thriving (and healing) as a single parent	116
9 Practical tips for managing single-parent life	130
10 How to support a single parent	139
Epilogue: A look into the future	143
Resources	149
References	151
Index	155

'You have totally got this. You are capable of far more than you could ever possibly imagine right now. You can move mountains and you will.'
Becky James

Introduction

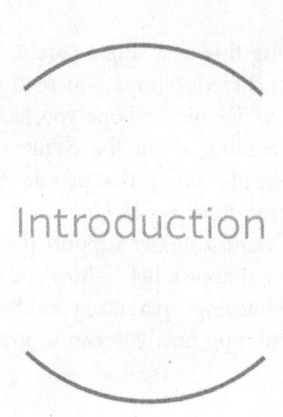

Hi. What brought you here? If you're feeling anything like the many single parents I have spoken to over the last year, I'm guessing it's because you're hoping to read or listen to something about single parenting that isn't a negative headline or focuses on all the things you need to do. Perhaps something that makes you feel seen and understood? Maybe you're here because you support parents, or someone in your life is a single parent and you want to learn more. Perhaps you just want to understand this experience of parenting better. Whoever you are and whyever you are here, welcome.

This book is all about single parents. I deliberately chose that title rather than single *parenting*, because I wanted this to be about better understanding, sharing and validating the experiences of single parents. Naturally we're going to talk about supporting children too, but most of the book is about how we support those doing the caring. It's about highlighting the many different journeys that lead to someone becoming a single parent, the visible and not-so-visible impacts of that, and how we can all help play a role in supporting them.

If you're reading this as a single parent, I hope this book makes you feel included. I hope you read or listen to parts and think *'that's so like me!'*. I hope you feel reassurance and validation from reading about the challenges other parents have faced, or unhelpful things that people say (you know, like *'I wish I got a break from my children too'*). If you're reading this because you want to better support the single parents in your life, thank you. I hope it helps show you some of the many varied experiences of single parenting and how they can feel. I also hope the section on how you can support a single parent is useful.

Who do we define as a single parent?

According to the last count by the Office of National Statistics in the UK, there are almost 3 million single parents in the UK, or around one in six families with a child under 18. Most of those parents are female and most are the biological mother to their children. But there are many different types of single parent and varied stories of how they became one. Some will have become a single parent through choice, perhaps as an adoptive parent or via IVF. Others will have sadly lost a partner. Many will have had a difficult past relationship with their child's other parent, although sometimes partners grow apart amicably, or did not really know each other in the first place.

One of the most common questions I hear on this topic is *'but what actually counts as a single parent?'*. It can be really tempting to start comparing different scenarios, as a sort of 'hierarchy of difficulty' of single parenting, but I don't think that's particularly helpful, for many reasons. Although some situations may appear more difficult than others on paper, we're not single parents in a bubble. Our broader experiences including finances, health, and other relationships can really affect our experience of single parenting.

Introduction

To me, the core part of being a single parent is that your child's other parent is not around to share the load of caring for your child and being part of your family day to day. Clearly, the scenarios mentioned above are all very different and will be driven by different complex emotions, different past experiences and differences in current potential support. Despite that, however, there is something uniting about the experience of single parenting – perhaps a shared understanding of what it is like to not have someone else that you love and care for sharing the day-to-day responsibility of caring for your child.

Of course, many single parents will go on to start a new relationship. As we will see later, that can be a very positive experience, or it can add further complexities. However, even when a new partner is very hands-on, loving, and takes on some of the mental load, I think many single parents still feel, to varying degrees, a greater responsibility for their child. New relationships can throw up all sorts of strange financial and support complexities too. Although some couples might see themselves as two parents, others feel that they are still a single parent but in a relationship.

Some single parents will have an ex-partner who still supports their children. As we know, this experience can vary hugely. It might range from a genuinely shared load of emotional, practical and financial support, through to occasional visits or sketchy financial support payments. Others will not have any support, due to a partner disappearing, refusing to pay or because of bereavement. Some people prefer to refer to parenting without another parent or adult present as 'solo parenting'.

Relationships between co-parents can also vary greatly. Sometimes two parents get along even better than before in a co-parenting relationship. They are caring, friendly and supportive of each other. Conversely, some will continue to experience emotional and financial abuse from an ex-partner who remains in their life due to their child. Some might be in the middle, trying to stay civil and friendly to maintain stability for their children.

I'm not quite done yet, though (see why this gets complicated?). Throw in other elements that intersect with the experience of being a single parent, such as whether you have the support of a close-knit family who take a hands-on role, money, work, health, disability, wellbeing, the religious and cultural views of people around you… and generally, it just becomes really hard to say that experiences can be 'ranked' in some way. Everyone's situation is different, but that core aspect of no longer living with, or never having had a relationship with the other or another parent of your child, is what single parents have in common.

I'll come back to this later, but I want to make a note on the common suggestion that someone can 'feel like a single parent' because their partner works long hours, works away, or despite living in the same house doesn't play an active role. Those are all really tough situations and deserving of support in their own ways, but they're distinctly different from single parenting. Sadly, of course, some people will be in relationships in which their partner does not contribute equally or at all to the financial, emotional and practical load of parenting. However, doing the day-to-day care for your children alone, but having financial and emotional support from your child's other parent, is different to single parenting.

My attempts to describe what a single parent is clearly show the depth and diversity of who single parents are. I have my own experiences of separation and single parenting, but I am just one person, and I wanted to bring a variety of different voices to this book. So I invited 17 parents with experience of

Introduction

single parenting, from different backgrounds, to share their experiences and supportive messages. Alongside exploring their journey to single parenthood, I asked them about the challenges they faced and things that helped them. I hope that if you are a single parent reading this book, you find something of yourself in these stories, and I'm sorry that I couldn't cover every single scenario. As we go through the book I've tried to balance information and support as it applies to relationship breakdown, bereavement and choice. Although I think a lot of the content applies across scenarios, there will be some information and sections directed towards each of these contexts.

Meet the contributors

<u>Becky</u> is a 38-year-old mother of four and lives in Cambridgeshire. Her children were 11, 8, 4 and 3 when she became a single parent. They are 14, 11, 7 and 6 now. Becky describes her marriage as slowly breaking down over three years. After numerous failed attempts to fix things, she finally decided it was a lost cause and ended the relationship. Her husband moved out, fortunately just before lockdown.

<u>Craig</u> is 38 and white Scottish. He separated from his children's mother when their children were aged 5 and 3. Craig does the majority of caring for his children as their mother has experienced significant mental health challenges, which mean she struggles with day-to-day care. She sees her children two to three times per month, depending on her health. He is in a long-term relationship but they chose to live separately as they didn't want to move their children's schools.

<u>Dan</u> is 48 years old, mixed race (Black African and white French) and lives in London. He was a stay-at-home father for several years before his relationship broke down. He has a

flexible shared-care relationship with his ex-partner, and has his children a little more than half of the time, mainly due to her working patterns. His son is now 11 years old and his daughter is 9, and Dan and his partner separated five years ago. He remarried two years ago, to a woman who has a son who is now 12. Her ex-partner rarely sees their son.

Elizabeth has an 11-year-old daughter. She is a writer and for the past few years has been a full-time carer, living with her 96-year-old mother who was recently diagnosed with dementia. She became a single parent not long after her daughter was born. Her ex-husband became abusive during pregnancy, and it got worse during the first year of her daughter's life. For both of their safety they moved out.

Evangeline is 43 and has two teenagers. She separated from her children's father when she was pregnant with her second baby. He has little consistent contact with his children, sometimes appearing back in their lives and often doing more harm than good with these sporadic and often emotionally avoidant encounters. Evangeline has remarried and is happy in her relationship, and has also become stepmother to two similarly aged children.

Hayley is 48 years old, white, and a mother to one teenage daughter, living in Bristol. She was widowed 12 years ago when she was living abroad. Her husband was diagnosed with terminal bowel cancer in his thirties when their daughter was a toddler. She did much of his medical care at home in the last few months of his life as well as trying to care for their daughter. He died at home less than a year after diagnosis. Hayley had also lost her own mum when she was in her early twenties. Her daughter is now 14 years old and Hayley met

Introduction

her new partner around four years after she was widowed. He moved in about two years later.

<u>Jennie</u> is 41, lives in Cardiff, and is a single parent to one child who is now 20. She now has two stepdaughters too. She is white Welsh and was diagnosed with ADHD at 39, which explained a lot! She is what in America is known as 'twice exceptional', which is a huge barrier to any recognition of neurodiversity. Jennie was a single parent from when she was a few months pregnant, after a very short relationship resulted in pregnancy. She is now married and has two stepchildren, marrying when her daughter was 9. Prior to that she had had a live-in partner for some of the years in between, although she did most of the 'parenting' herself.

<u>Jess</u> is 45, a mother to a teenage son, and lives in Wales. She has been a single parent for 10 years, having divorced her abusive husband after many years of being unhappy in the relationship. She was 34 when she divorced and her son, who was 6 years old at the time, is now 16. Jess works full-time and has done since returning from maternity leave.

<u>Karyn</u> is a 47-year-old solo adopter of one daughter, who is 4½ years old. Karyn adopted her when she was 11 months old. Her daughter experienced early years developmental trauma and significant losses in respect of her birth parents and foster carers, resulting in her struggling to manage and make sense of her emotions and transitions. Karyn was originally planning to have IVF treatment to become a parent, but her now ex-partner then told her that he didn't want a child. After ending the relationship and taking some time out, including having fertility counselling, she made the decision around 10 months later to apply to become a single adopter.

Why Single Parents Matter

<u>Kirstie</u> is 48 and lives in London with her two teenage children. She separated from her son's father when the children were in primary school, due to the combination of him working very long hours and committing adultery numerous times on work nights out. Their relationship has never recovered although he does provide financial support. He sees his children approximately once a month when it suits his business schedule. Kirstie has been living with her new partner for two years.

<u>Lauren</u> separated from her long-term partner Sarah when their daughter was 5 years old. She is now 11. At first Sarah remained an active parent, but over time she found this too challenging and moved away and is no longer involved. Lauren knew her child's father, who was an old friend, and he is involved as a supportive figure in their lives despite living in the USA. Lauren has actively chosen not to find a new partner for now.

<u>Martha</u> is 35 and a mother of two boys, from North Yorkshire. Her son was 3 months old when she left his father, and he is 7 years old now. Her relationship was very tumultuous and once their son came along the couple found their parenting ideas were too different. Martha remained in an on/off relationship with her ex-partner for some time, being strung along and finding it hard to let go. Later, once she'd spent time away from the isolation of living with him, and accessed therapy, she realised she had been in an emotionally and financially abusive relationship. She met her new partner in 2019 and he moved into their home in 2021. They now have a child of their own.

<u>Nicole</u> is 38 years old and a single mother to two children who are now aged 11 and 14. She is educated to Masters level and

runs three successful businesses. She is Black from Caribbean descent and has faced adversity, particularly in the workplace as she has tried to progress in her career. She has a strong work ethic and is fiercely determined to change this narrative for her daughters, so she decided to set up her own company to fulfil her goals for her family. She became a single parent when she was pregnant with her second child, after a 10-year history of domestic, emotional and financial abuse.

Pete, aged 42, lives in Derbyshire with his wife Nicola and their three children. Pete was widowed when his children were 3 years and 10 weeks old. He met his current wife in 2013, when they became friends, but they didn't get together as a couple until several years later, at which point she was working abroad. As soon as she came back she moved straight in with Pete and three months later they bought a house together. Their baby Flynn was born 6 months later, and the couple married in 2019.

Rachel is 39, and is mixed Chinese and white British. She gave birth to her son, who was conceived via IVF using donor sperm, three years ago. She made the decision after her partner passed away from bowel cancer when they were both 32. She did not know whether she would want another serious relationship, but was very keen to have a child and felt that time was not on her side. She felt becoming a single parent by choice was the right decision for her. She has not yet had another relationship but does not rule it out.

Rebecca is 48, white and has two teenage children. She separated from her child's father when the children were 5 and 7. She is now remarried to a man who had two slightly younger children, and things are finally more amicable with her ex-husband, particularly in recent years after he remarried too. Things were very difficult immediately after they split due to his affair and his reluctance to leave the family home.

Stacey is 26 and lives in Scotland with her son who is now 7 years old. She had a short relationship with her child's father but they separated before her son was born. They have a friendly but distant relationship. Her son's father has a lot of challenges in life and although he does see his son this can be sporadic, and he sometimes needs additional support in caring for him. Stacey moved in with her partner, who doesn't yet have children, around a year ago. They are expecting a baby together in a few months.

I've structured this book in three parts. The first explores how it feels to be a single parent, including examining the evidence behind the headlines claiming that single parenting negatively affects children (spoiler: it really doesn't, but a lack of support can make it difficult for you). The second part dives into some of the challenges you might experience: supporting your child, co-parenting, finances, and new relationships. The third part brings together ideas from the contributors to dig into what can help you thrive as a single parent and how others can help. We finish with a look into the future, or rather, we hear some messages from the grown-up children of single parents reflecting on what their single parents did well and thanking them for it all.

PART I
HOW DOES IT FEEL TO BE A SINGLE PARENT?

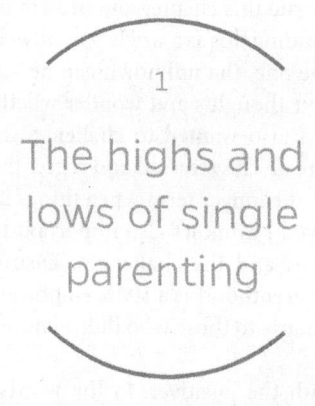

1
The highs and lows of single parenting

What's it really like to be a single parent? Is it like the headlines say – something terrible to be avoided at all costs – or is it actually a little bit more complicated than that? Could it, just possibly, even be *better* in some cases, in both the short and long term? Is there just one experience of single parenting, or do people bring their backgrounds, lives and personalities to it, resulting in situations that are far more diverse than any headline could describe? After all, what does it feel like to be in a two-parent household?

When I asked the parents who contributed to this book what it felt like to be a single parent, the responses were naturally mixed – as you might expect from a group of parents who had taken diverse pathways to single parenthood. Just as with any type of parenting there were often positives and silver linings, challenges, and a whole load of mixed emotions going on. Context really mattered. Adultery, abuse, bereavement, infertility and more may all bring about very different experiences than for those who entered this space more amicably or through choice.

I wanted to write this chapter and present it first because I think if you're reading this as a single parent, or are imminently about to become one, the unknown can be scary. You might feel alone in your thoughts and wonder whether anyone else feels the same. I also wanted to challenge the idea that all single parents are always stressed and regret their life choices. Many, at least in the longer term when things have settled, are thriving. However, I think it's also important to acknowledge the raw emotions and the challenges. Dismissing these or painting single parenthood as a 100% empowering experience is unfair, particularly to those who didn't choose or want to be in this place.

Let's start with the positives, in the words of our parent contributors.

1. The positives and silver linings
Freedom from the past and to make decisions.

'Free. I was so glad to be free. At first there was always the thought in the back of my mind that we could rekindle, and I think I held onto this while healing. When he got married to his now partner that's when I was truly free, and the stored emotions and trauma were released from within. My girls have so much love, trust and respect for me and vice versa. We make decisions together, we have great communication, and we don't have the other parent's baggage and/or ways of parenting conflicting. It's worked out to be the best thing that could have happened for our family' Nicole

The highs and lows of single parenting

Realising that you're in a better place.

'Becoming a single parent was an overwhelmingly positive experience. Mostly this was due to the freedom we had in our lives as a result without feeling controlled, having a bad atmosphere in the house or feeling trapped and resentful. I was very concerned about money and being solely responsible for the bills and having enough money to last each month. However, I quickly discovered that I was financially better off on my own with having control over the monthly expenditure. I have times now when I feel sad that my son does not have a father figure in his life, however I believe that this is better than the influence his father would have had on him.' Jess

Feeling like you can parent 'better' than before.

'I'm less stressed, calmer and happier and that definitely rubs off on how I parent.' Craig

Not having to compromise on what's important.

'I very much felt that being a single parent had some big positives – in that I could parent in the way I felt was right! I didn't have to debate that or compromise with anyone. I do absolutely see there are benefits to having someone else's input, and I did have a lot of friends and family around for that, but it was much easier to maintain consistency with one parent with the same rules and boundaries.' Jennie

A deeper connection to your children.

'We get to enjoy so much more time together, we are very close and talk about everything. Being a single mum has allowed me so much joy, holidays just the two of us, holding hands on the school run, midnight feasts,

> *learning from her, working out how to make the pennies last the week together, celebrating achievements, walking in the woods, jumping in puddles, and just knowing someone else so well.'* Elizabeth

Gaining new friends.

> *'I gained lots of friends through having a child and I think being a single parent actually enhanced that – it meant I would be at children's activities etc alone so would get talking to others and was more likely to be available to socialise with my child at other times like weekends, when other people would be with partners!'* Jennie

And for some… getting to experience parenthood their way.

> *'Lots of amazing positives, we have an incredible bond, experienced love in a completely different way. Seeing the world through my daughter's eyes, e.g. being amazed at the world and wanting to learn and understand the world. Seeing her smile and laugh, gaining confidence and making and maintaining friendships – seeing the things that she may have struggled with due to her early years but to see her thriving, healthy and happy.* Karyn (single adopter)

> *'I couldn't see myself being ready for a serious relationship any time soon and when I started to calculate how old I might be even if I did find another partner in the not-so-distant future I was worried it would be too late. Mike and I had always discussed having children and it felt like I was carrying out his wishes by me becoming a mother even though he wasn't here, and the baby sadly wasn't his.'* Rachel (solo IVF)

2. The difficult parts

Of course, single parenting, like any parenting, or indeed anything in life, is not always straightforward. One of the main themes that came out when talking to parents was that single parenting could bring up a lot of different and difficult emotions. This did not necessarily mean that parents who had separated from a partner or become a single parent by choice felt regret, but more that life as a single parent had specific difficulties. However, many felt pride at managing these alone, often stressing that it was still better than the alternative. Naturally, for those brought to single parenting through bereavement, parenting experiences were so closely caught up with the complex and difficult emotions of bereavement that it was hard to disentangle the two. In these cases, positive emotions or experiences could ignite guilt.

Feeling the pressure.

> *'The juggling of childcare and work. It being all on me 24/7 and having no respite ever. The mental strain and the financial strain… but somehow, I've made it this far. Quite incredible really.'* Nicole

Feeling nervous about the future.

> *'I worry a lot about how I will cope in the future alone when bills get bigger or my daughter has more complex needs as a teenager.'* Lauren

Feelings of loss at what could have been.

> *'I sometimes feel a sense of regret or loss at what could have been had his behaviour been different. I look at my friends who have the support of their partner and can feel angry at him being unable to do that.'* Kirstie

Why Single Parents Matter

Or loss of doing things differently.

> 'The loss of not being a birth parent doesn't disappear when you adopt; there are triggers and I manage them, but it doesn't take away the feelings of loss, e.g. seeing pregnant women, seeing women breastfeeding, couples with a newborn baby, etc. Karyn

Always having to be the one who sets the rules.

> 'Sometimes it feels as if I would like someone to play bad cop at times, as I have to be disciplinarian and comforter. That can be overwhelming but so far we have worked a way through emotional ups and downs'. Elizabeth

Supporting your children's emotions when you are hurting too.

> 'Having to shelve my own pain and trauma to deal with theirs first, then finding time to process mine so that it doesn't spill out at random moments.' Becky

The lack of adult company.

> 'I found it difficult not to have adult company in the evening or on the weekends/holidays which seemed to all be about family time. No one wanted me tagging along.' Evangeline

And feeling that other parents can't relate.

> 'Not all of my friends get it and sometimes moan to me about partners or the pressures of being a dad in a couple. It's hard to bite your tongue sometimes.' Craig

Not being able to fix things for your children.

> 'Not being able to share it with the person who had given birth to them and help them because in my mind

practically no matter how good a Dad I am you cannot replace Mair's feel, touch, smell, skin texture and more so a Mummy cuddle cannot be replaced.' Pete

The overwhelm.

'The most challenging thing from a practical perspective when I was first widowed was dealing with all the legal paperwork, going through probate, never-ending decisions and all the stuff that needed to be organised which led to feelings of paralysis and overwhelm.' Hayley

Feeling guilt at positive experiences.

'Although Theo is not Mike's baby, I sometimes feel guilt for enjoying aspects of parenting on my own. When you're a single parent by choice you don't have to consider anyone else's preferred ways of parenting or put up with how they do things differently. Don't get me wrong, it's hard, but I also like that freedom and that sometimes leads to guilt as I wouldn't have this freedom if he hadn't died.' Rachel

Parents also talked about financial challenges, learning how to support their child, and navigating difficulties such as poor relationships and loss. These are discussed in detail in Part II.

3. The frustrations

Another aspect of single parenting is putting up with the frankly daft comments people seem to idly make about being a single parent. Although I'm sure many of these come from a place of kindness, an attempt to empathise, or are simply small talk, this doesn't stop them being deeply frustrating. If you're a single parent, I hope this section at least makes you feel less alone. If you're reading it to support others, here's the long explanation for why these small phrases matter.

'I often feel like a single parent too.'

> 'People used to say their partner working away a lot or not helping out at home made them feel like a single parent which was very upsetting as it dismissed the reality that those fathers were usually financially contributing and/or were available at other times for childcare etc.' Martha

This must be one of the most common phrases uttered to single parents, often by other parents who spend considerable time parenting their children alone, but who are in a relationship. There are so many differences, subtle and otherwise, between the two experiences and it can be a really tricky one to try and explain.

This isn't about parenting top trumps. The world isn't a simple place, and anyone's experience of parenting is affected by so many different factors. I'm certainly not saying that every single parent has it tougher than all parents who are in relationships. In fact, many single parents are shocked by the fact that single parenting can feel easier if it comes at the end of a difficult relationship. But it is still *different*.

> 'There is nobody else with the same responsibility and love for my son to talk through perspectives on the day-to-day challenges or successes. I have almost no feedback on whether the approach I take with parenting is reasonable or sensible or if I should try something else.' Jess

Single parenting is about more than the act of practically caring for children day-to-day. Often it seems that even when your child's other partner is involved in co-parenting, the main responsibilities fall to you with no one who you can hold equally responsible (even if they don't actually do anything). There's no income coming in from anyone else to fall back on. Or a partner to chat to (or rant at) at the end of the day about how frustrating the day has been, even if it's by text message. There can often be a huge feeling of just being... *alone* in it all.

> *'It isn't just a case of him not being there, but I feel I must make up for the feelings of rejection and that lack of a reassuring love. That's what I find more difficult – practically caring for him isn't as difficult in comparison.'*
> Stacey

There can be a phenomenal feeling of weight of responsibility that you are the only one who will be there for your children: physically, financially, and emotionally. In many cases you might feel the need to make up the shortfall in these things, particularly emotional stability. This can feel overwhelming.

> *'I was surprised to find the feelings of responsibility didn't go away when my partner moved in; he didn't have the same default responsibility that I did.'* Evangeline

You might expect that if a single parent goes on to have a new relationship, and especially if they live with their partner, these feelings will go away. Although to some extent they do reduce, often they don't completely disappear because of that default feeling of responsibility Evangeline describes above. There is more on this in the relationships chapter, but even a great partner often doesn't carry the same weight as a co-parent. You may feel that your child is not actually their responsibility, so you end up taking on more, or feeling that you can't ask them to do tedious or time-consuming things in the same way you might of the child's other parent.

Of course – these things can be missing in relationships too. You might have a partner who refuses to or is unable to work, or who you can't share your feelings with. Or who works away all the time, or long hours. Maybe they are abusive or create more work. These are all tough situations, but they're different from single parenting. Everyone needs support – it's not about a 'hierarchy of toughness' – but differentiating between situations is important so that parents feel seen, and the right support is explored.

'I'm so jealous of the time you get away from your children'.

'I often had to force myself to make plans when the kids were at their dad's. I missed them so much and felt really unsettled and anxious when they weren't here. If I didn't make plans I would mope around the house, doom scroll on social media or get really panicky. To the outside world it probably looked like I was out having a brilliant time, but in reality it was a coping strategy to try and pass the time until they were back with me.' Rebecca

Oof. This is a big one. Many primary single parents who share parenting with a former partner have an arrangement where children visit their other parent every other weekend (and sometimes one night in the week). Theoretically, this means that the primary single parent has every other weekend 'off' – time to party, right?! Although this can look like a very appealing set-up for those who rarely have a break from their children, the reality is often very different.

One of the most frustrating parts of parenting is that you often spend time wishing for something to happen or change, and then once it happens you miss the old version. This can apply tenfold to the 'break' from single parenting. For those who don't get a regular break from childcare as they live with

The highs and lows of single parenting

their child's other parent, time away from their children can feel like a wonderful thing or a luxury. The reality, however, when you are sharing care of children, is that you don't always like or trust the other parent. There may be a history of abuse (that may be ongoing), which feels like a punch in the stomach every time you have to hand your child over. You might worry about how the other parent will care for the children, or how the children will be feeling. And the worst bit is that there is very little scope for you to control this. Requests can of course be made, but often they are ignored (sometimes deliberately, to upset you), leaving you feeling unsettled and guilty at not being there for your children. It's not the same as leaving them with a trusted family member or carer.

'When they were younger the children were really difficult in the day or so after they came back from his. He usually let them run wild, hadn't bothered with sensible bedtimes and filled them full of sugar.' Kirstie

A common tactic, often described online, is for fathers who spend little time with their children to become 'Disney Dads' (I'm sure 'Disney Mums' exist too, but if you google 'Disney Mum' you get a list of cartoon characters). A Disney Dad tends to let children do whatever they want, eat whatever they want and go to bed whenever they feel like it. There are few rules, little disagreement and lots and lots of fun activities. Meals out? Water skiing? A new toy? Sure! This is all far more affordable in terms of both money and energy when you're not paying for the mundane day-to-day reality of caring for children the other 12 out of 14 days.

'Sharing care felt like he had control over me still. I never knew whether he would turn up to take them or cancel

> *at the last minute, so if I made any plans for those couple of days I felt anxious in the run-up, wondering whether he would stick to his word. He was often "ill" or returned them to me early on a whim. Of course, I could never do the same in return, it was an unspoken rule that his home was not really their home. Although he did see them it always felt like he had the option to do it or not and I was the default parent.'* Evangeline

In the UK there is no law in place that says that separated parents must commit a certain amount of time to provide care for their children (unless specifically stated in a court order and that gets tricky – there's more on this in Chapter 5). Theoretically, if they commit to less care, their financial contributions should rise in line with child maintenance rates. However, as we will explore later in Chapter 6, that is often not the reality, and situations are too complex to keep recontacting the other parent to change details. This means that many of those co-parenting are left dependent on the person they once had a relationship with simply keeping their word. Of course, there are many great co-parents who are reliable and supportive. Sadly there are many others who use child contact as a means to continue controlling their ex-partner.

> *'People used to think I was having a luxurious weekend, but the reality was that I spent most of it catching up on all the things I couldn't do because I was the only adult available most of the time. Housework, shopping, filling in forms – it wasn't exactly a spa weekend.'* Kirstie

This is another aspect that is often overlooked. Although again there are of course exceptions and variations among couples, when you are the sole adult in your household, all

The highs and lows of single parenting

the responsibility for housework and life admin tends to fall to you. When your children are small and you're home for the evening, there is little chance to just pop back out to the shops or run an errand or go to the gym. At home there are far fewer opportunities for the space and quiet to get things done. There's no one to take over bathtime or keep an eye on dinner while you get on with other things. All the questions get asked of you.

> *'I found that somehow, I was still doing parenting when they weren't here. He'd message asking basic questions and once they were old enough to have phones, they'd be messaging and contacting me all the time too. I was still parenting, just they were in a different location which when they were teens didn't feel that different to the weeks they were with me. It meant I didn't ever properly switch off from my role of mum. Obviously he didn't experience the same when they were with me...'* Rebecca

Yes – although your children may well not be in your physical care for a weekend or an evening, that doesn't mean they simply disappear out of your mind. As Rebecca describes above, you're probably running about sorting out things related to them. You may well be in frequent contact with them, especially with older children who have phones. You most certainly will be thinking about them or worrying about whether they're okay.

And finally, we have the charming 'you're so lucky that their other parent is still involved'. As Kirstie exclaimed: 'A friend commented that at least their dad still saw them. Yes, once a month often for less than 48 hours. Clearly, we shared the parenting load!'

'Well, you chose to become a single parent'.

> *'I was in tears once over the stress and frustration of it all. I offloaded to my mother, and she replied that this was the downside of CHOOSING to be a single parent. I was incredulous. If I had stayed married things would have been even more difficult, but this didn't make this option easy. My choice would have been my husband keeping his vows and putting his family first. Yet again single mothers being blamed for the actions of a man.'* Evangeline

> *'Yes I chose single parenthood but that doesn't mean it was a fair choice. It also doesn't make it any less difficult. Am I glad I chose to do it over likely remaining childless? Of course! Does that mean I don't need support or things aren't overwhelming sometimes? Obviously not! Thankfully most of my friends and family understood this and those who didn't I distanced myself from.'* Rachel

Sometimes a parent chooses to become a single parent from the start, through IVF or adoption. Other times they might choose to end a difficult relationship because of the damage it is doing to themselves and their children. Are these simple choices? Does deciding to do something prevent any negatives? Should you carry all the responsibility and never express any negative emotions because you took control of a situation? No, no and no.

'I don't know how you do it'.

> *'I struggle with the comments of "you are amazing doing that, I could never do it" or "your daughter is so lucky to have you" (no she isn't, she has been through trauma which will have a long-lasting impact on her).'* Karyn

The highs and lows of single parenting

This one is often so well-meaning, but can be frustrating. I think it applies to a lot of challenging parenting circumstances, such as having a child with additional needs or illness, or if you are unwell yourself. You 'do it' because there really isn't a lot of choice, is there?

> *'People are always making comments about how amazing I am to be a single parent or how difficult it must be for me. I think there are hard bits but there are things that are a lot easier too! I don't like people making that assumption.'* Jennie

Of course, for others, their experience of single parenting is actually easier than it was being in that particular relationship. Feeling that others are pitying you or overstating what you do can feel uncomfortable.

As you can see from this chapter, the experience of single parenting varies according to circumstances. Just like parenting in a two-parent household, there are joys, tensions and frustrations. There is no single experience of single parenting – whatever the media portrays – and many find great relief, connection and happiness in parenting alone, albeit in between eyerolling at the unthinking things people can say. This leaves us with the question – where did the idea that single parenting is a solely challenging experience come from?

2

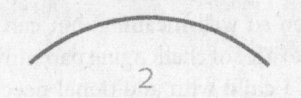

Where did the stereotypes about single parenting come from?

> 'I don't read the papers, and anything negative doesn't have an impact as it's not my story so I don't believe their narrative.' Nicole

If you're a single parent, I bet that you're very aware of the unhelpful headlines and media stereotypes that pop up about single parenting. A quick search of recent tabloid headlines informs me that teens of single parents are more likely to get involved in graffiti (not Banksy-esque I assume), someone or other doesn't want to date a single mother, and young women are being enticed into single parenting due to all those financial benefits. Strangely, even though I deliberately searched for single 'parents', every single headline talks about mothers, and often younger ones at that. It's almost as if there is an agenda. Just in case sarcasm doesn't work in print – there absolutely is an agenda and it's been around for a long time.

I can poke fun at these ridiculous headlines, but it remains a serious issue. A core worry that single parents often have is whether their children will be affected by not living in a two-parent household, and this type of headline and political comment exacerbates those fears. Let me reassure you. If you are reading this as a single parent, then the short version, before we get into the detail, is that the chances are that your children will be just fine. More than fine. They will thrive, mostly because the very fact that you are concerned about them shows that you're acing parenting. They are loved and they are cared for and at the end of the day that is what matters.

Of course, there will likely be challenges. I don't want to patronise you by saying it's all going to be great and smooth sailing. Experiences of separation and bereavement can be extraordinarily tough, but it's important to separate out challenging experiences, for which you can seek support for your children (and yourself), and the act of single parenting itself. There is no evidence that simply being part of a single-parent household damages children in any way. We'll come back to the topic of supporting your child through change in Chapter 4, but for now I want to remind you that *all* families have challenges… it's just that the media, politicians, and others with an agenda like to encourage the idea that single parenthood is a disaster. And if your child is struggling with something in their lives, it doesn't mean in the slightest that it's *because* you are a single parent. Children struggle with all sorts of things and in fact may have been struggling even more if you had stayed in a difficult relationship. The next chapter will examine the *actual* evidence about the impact of single parenting (spoiler: it certainly doesn't match these ridiculous headlines), but first I want to look at how we ended up with the idea that single parenting is a negative thing.

Stereotypes and the single mother

'The headlines ignore the very real, nuanced and complex

issues around solo parenting. They usually focus on how terrible the mother is rather than the absent or less available father. We're seen as sponges or chavvy, or broken and damaged. There's also a lot of victim blaming of abuse survivors.' Martha

To understand where these headlines and misconceptions come from, it's useful to delve briefly into the history of how they developed and why. Attitudes towards single-parent families have changed and evolved over the years. Without making this an entire book about the injustice of historic attitudes and treatment of single mothers in particular, it is fair to say that law-makers and societies of the past have done a great deal of harm. I use the word mother here because most of the negative views of single parenting are aimed at women. This is in part because most single parents are women, but also because of misogyny targeted at women in these situations.

'I've met people who hold negative views of single parents, painting them all as lazy or undeserving of support. When they find out I was a single parent for many years they backtrack and say "oh but not you, that's different", presumably meaning it's all ok for me because I was a slightly older mother and have a good job. It enrages me.'
Rebecca

Furthermore, the focus has tended to be on mothers in a particular situation – younger, with less money and separated from their child's other parent. I have completely failed to find an equivalent array of articles criticising men who do not play an equal role in raising their children. Additionally, rarely do articles focus on older mothers, and they also tend to ignore any research exploring the concept of single parenting by choice. Yet somehow, some people feel that these headlines and associated beliefs are acceptable, encouraging 'othering' behaviour and stereotyping without stopping to consider the impact of their views.

Conversely, as you will see from the experiences of many of the male single parents in this book, men rarely experience this same negativity. In fact, they often have praise heaped upon them or numerous offers of help. Many men find this harmful in a different way – it's condescending and belittling, and frustrating if they are aware of the inequitable treatment of their fellow female single parents. As Pete explained:

> *'Judgement crept in from some quarters that "wasn't I doing amazingly given what's happened" and I found this made me quite prickly because I was doing a lot of what I would have been if Mair was still here. I didn't become Dad overnight because my wife was ill or died. I did this anyway. I was just a doer'.*

Dan, who was a stay-at-home parent for many years before his divorce felt similarly:

> *'I thought it was bad enough when I was still married. All the comments about how good a job I was doing. My female friends doing the same thing didn't get that response! But when people find out I'm the main resident parent for two children something funny happens to their brains. You'd think I'd solved world peace.'*

The history of single motherhood

The following sections are written from the perspective of the UK and Ireland, but attitudes and experiences were similar in many other countries.

If we look back over the last century we can see clear trends in how single parenting (typically mothers) has been presented. Although many single mothers today have experienced hostility or judgement from others, it is fair to say that things have thankfully come a long way compared to how single mothers were treated in the pre-war era and the decades that followed. In religious, financial and legal terms (such as illegitimacy – which wasn't removed until 1987!), pregnancy outside marriage was considered a shameful sin, with that judgement directed solely at the mother-to-be, as if she had somehow magically got herself pregnant. Women and girls were often thrown out of families, or hidden and then sent away to give birth, give their baby up for adoption and return as if nothing had happened. Sometimes babies were passed off as belonging to a grandmother or older married sister to keep them in the family. Ultimately, without a family prepared to support them (and few would at the time due to the stigma), adoption was the only answer as there was no financial support net, or any services set up to support single parents.[1]

If they were not supported by their family, mothers were often forced into workhouses.[2] Others left their children in the care of institutions such as the Foundling Hospital, which gave mothers the option to leave their children to be cared for while they went away to try to establish themselves with a job and place to live.[3] When a mother left her child, their name was changed but the mother could leave a small token of identification which would be given back when she collected her child. The Foundling Museum set up to remember the institution sadly has many hundreds of these tokens, often handmade, demonstrating that mothers were often never able to return to collect their children.

The Foundling Hospital was unusual in its time, although the concept of responsibility for caring for those without money had been around since the 1500s and expanded during the reign of Elizabeth I. The introduction of the Poor Law in 1601 required that those without means be offered work or support in some way, and that this should be funded through taxes. It was driven by the idea that the poor would organise riots and crime, with many sent to harsh workhouses and kept away from society. But it was the beginning of the idea of formalised state responsibility.[4]

In the 1920s the concept of the welfare state, in which a government must take on the responsibility to support those unable to support themselves, really started to develop. In 1925 it was decided that mothers who were widowed should be given financial support (10 shillings a week for life, with children also receiving money until they were 14).[5] Unfortunately, despite the small sums involved, this terrified governments and religious groups of the time into thinking that this support would encourage women to have babies out of wedlock or families to separate. The decision was made that unmarried or divorced mothers would not be allowed this support, as if this would work as a deterrent. The policy did not account for the fact that pregnancy (or remaining in a marriage) was not solely the choice of the woman.

However, in the eyes of those in parliament (i.e. men), not having access to this money was not seen as *enough* of a deterrent. A campaign of stigma and shame around single motherhood was created, supposedly to maintain the family unit, uphold the perceived 'moral' value of babies being born in marriage, and ultimately reduce reliance on the state. Women (held solely responsible for pregnancy, remember) had to be stopped from seeing pregnancy outside of marriage as a 'reward', and making a spectacle of those who dared to do this was seen as the way forward. At no point was this ever to do with any established evidence about negative outcomes for children of single parents. However, if you plunge women into a life of shame and poverty, you can quickly do some back calculations to suggest that any negative outcomes are solely due to her not being married.

Without adequate financial support, pregnant unmarried women whose families would not hide or support their pregnancies were housed in hostels designed for unmarried mothers and their babies. These hostels were often funded and run by churches and the Salvation Army. Writing for the *Guardian*,[6] in an article entitled '*Sin and the single mother: The history of lone parenthood*' back in 2012, Maureen Paton, who was born in the 1950s, describes her story of realising that she had been born in 'Birdhurst Lodge' – a grand-sounding place which was actually a mother and baby hostel.

In the UK unmarried pregnant mothers typically spent around three months in these hostels, half before they gave birth and for six weeks afterwards. During these six weeks they were required to decide whether they wanted to keep their baby or give them up for adoption to married childless couples, with heavy pressure to choose the latter, as how would they support their baby without an income (and with a whole heap of shame)? Often women were required to perform intense manual work while in these 'homes', with harsh living conditions. In the UK the last Salvation Army 'mother and baby home' was closed as late as 1980 and since then enquiries into the treatment of mothers and babies have been held. It is estimated that around 20,000 babies were born in Salvation Army homes from 1945–80, with around a third being adopted.

In Ireland, similar institutions existed, often run by Catholic nuns. Conditions were harsh and often unsanitary, leading to the spread of illness, and women were often worked hard. Adoption rates were high. Women had little option to keep their baby as Unmarried Mother's Allowance was not introduced until 1973. In 2015 the Irish Government conducted a judicial commission of investigation into these homes due to reports that up to 800 bodies of babies and children had been found in a mass grave at the Bon Secours mother and baby home. If you would like to read more, in-depth research was conducted by Queen's University Belfast and Ulster University into mother and baby homes and Magdalena laundries (similar institutions where women deemed to have 'sinned' were sent).[7]

Since the discoveries in Ireland, apologies have been made and investigations continue across the UK. However, the legacy of trauma and grief is deep and long-lasting, and something many women did not recover from. Given what we now know about intergenerational trauma, on an individual, family, and community level, from personal experiences and hearing stories, these events will continue to affect people today.

Changes in attitudes

Attitudes to supporting single mothers started to change around the time of the Second World War, but change was slow to come. In 1948 unmarried and divorced women were finally given a small amount of financial support, but things were still very difficult for them. They had reduced priority compared to couples for social housing until the 1977 Housing Act. But it was almost as if the more governments offered financial support, the more they also reinforced the vindictive view of single parents (mothers) being a scourge and drain on society (to reduce the need to follow through with the support). So determined were the politicians to try to prevent mothers from making the choice to be a single parent (presumably alone or by magic), that little thought was given to the impact on those already in that situation.

The number of single parents continued to increase as the decades passed, particularly as we hit the 1980s. Why? Well, it wasn't because a small financial security net made women run out and have babies on their own, planning to live off the state forever. Instead, it was because women no longer felt shamed or forced into giving up their babies for adoption, that they must immediately marry, or that they should stay with an abusive partner. Increased security for women through being able to work, having access to money, and better legal rights, gradually meant that more women could make decisions that were right for them. Some people will tell you that an increase in the number of single parents is a failure of society. I view it as the very opposite: it is a sign of women's increased autonomy, and that's before we even get into the freedom to consider solo IVF or adoption.

However, the increase in single parents really worried some people with strong 'traditional' religious or conservative views. There was a fear that the number of single parents would grow exponentially. The Thatcher government encouraged people to think that young girls were choosing single parenthood as a lifestyle option to get free money and free housing. Parliamentary debate records in 1993 show Peter Lilley, Minister for Social Security, referring to single mothers as 'benefit offenders', although he did also criticise the fathers who did not support them.[8] Meanwhile Tory MP Graham Riddick said 'When the welfare system encourages young women to have babies out of wedlock so that they can qualify for council houses and benefits, perhaps the system has gone too far?'. However, it was heartening to see Labour MP Glenda Jackson call this 'outrageous', stating 'there is absolutely no evidence whatever to support those scurrilous allegations'.

Where did the stereotypes come from?

Although those who are more critical thinkers will be able to see through the moral judgement masquerading as financial concern, the view that single parents are undeserving of financial support sadly persists. In one study exploring changes in British social attitudes to welfare spending from 1983–2012, single parents were regularly at the bottom of spending priorities. Notably, it isn't spending on children that people are averse to: almost three times as many people prioritised child benefit spending over single-parent support.[9]

Although attitudes are changing positively over time, some will still sadly encounter hostile views. The organisations Gingerbread www.gingerbread.org.uk and Single Parents Rights www.singleparentrights.org campaign for equality, support and an end to discrimination against single parents.

Before I get too carried away and write an entire book on the history of stigmatising single parents, let's have a look at what the evidence really says.

3

Is there any evidence that children from single-parent families have worse outcomes?

> 'Articles highlight that women/mothers are often seen as to blame for the way children are brought up, despite my experience being that my son's father should have far more judgement against him for failing in his duty as a parent.' Jess

If someone were to get their 'facts' from tabloid headlines they could very easily think that being part of a single-parent family causes all sorts of difficulties for children. But if we go to the actual research evidence and have a look, the story is very different. After searching over and over through hundreds of research papers it's clear to see that there is no strong evidence of a direct impact on children growing up in a single-parent household at all. As I mentioned in the previous chapter, I don't want to appear dismissive here of the challenges that can arise for children through separation and bereavement, and we will look specifically at supporting them through that in Chapter 4. However, the news headlines usually aren't talking about that; rather they imply that the experience of being single parented leads to negative outcomes, and that simply isn't true. When you look at the bigger picture, whether that's for educational achievement, behaviour or wellbeing, family structure has no significant impact.

The search took me so long because I was confused by the gap between the myths that circulate about single parenting and what the research was saying. What was clear, however, was how the social attitudes described in the last chapter really affected the direction of research. Back in the 1980s and 1990s, when social attitudes towards single parents were much more negative, it seemed that a lot of research (often conducted by men) sought to highlight the negative impact of single motherhood. A lot of these papers made sweeping statements about risk that were far stronger than the evidence suggested and failed to account for other broader factors such as poverty. It was eye-opening to read paper after paper directing blame at single mothers and their parenting, rather than considering that the real impact was that of poverty, typically caused by a lack of financial support from the father, a lack of structural support such as good childcare to enable mothers to work, and a general lack of a government safety net to nurture these families.

Once I limited my search to papers published only in the last 10–15 years, suddenly the tone changed. Research was far better conducted and often emphasised that once you considered lower incomes there was really no difference in outcomes at all. Authors were clearly stating that more financial support was needed, rather than blaming single mothers. On top of this there was a huge change in the direction of the research questions, particularly in terms of exploring the impact of single parenting on maternal mental health.

So what does the evidence say?

I've spent a long time thinking about this chapter and what it means and I want to say a few things before we get into the research.

1. I considered doing one of those 'look at this famous person, they had a single parent!' lists, but I purposefully decided not to. Why? Well, for a start most children do not go on to be famous. Although we might have high hopes of our child becoming rich and keeping us in a luxury lifestyle, it's probably not going to happen and that's okay. Success in life can mean many different things, not just fame.
2. Related to this, your child does not need to be some straight A, head girl, football team star to prove that you being a single parent didn't affect them. They can be a normal, average child, just like their friends who have two parents at home. They can struggle with stuff, make terrible choices and slam doors just like their friends. Sadly, we live in a world where rates of teenage mental health problems are increasing. It is far too easy, if your child struggles with something, to blame yourself as a single parent. However, many children within two-parent families will be struggling too. No one ever suggests that it's because they've got two parents at home.
3. You do not have to be some sort of super parent just because you are a single parent. Being a perfectly normal parent, making mistakes and having bad days is fine (more on this in Chapter 8).
4. Understanding the nuances of research and what they mean is important. As with any research, even if a study found that teenagers of single parents had an increased chance of depression for example, that doesn't mean that *a)* every child of a single parent will experience depression,

b) that the single parenting caused it, or *c)* that no child of a two-parent household will experience it. We also need to be able to look closely at what the increased risk is. Too often you will get a headline that overly simplifies research or is deliberately alarmist. If a study says that the risk doubles, we need to know what the risk was in the first place. If for example it was 5% and is now 10%, we know that there's still a 90% chance of it not happening. But media articles seem to love implying that any differences are huge and definitely to do with single parenting. And finally, research is not about individuals. Even if a study says that 'children are at higher risk', it doesn't tell you anything about your child. You are the expert on them. You do not need a study to prove that your child is happy and thriving.

Are there any established, high-impact detrimental outcomes of single parenting?

Short answer – no.

Longer answer – really, no. There are many published studies on the outcomes of children of single parents. Some find some evidence of an increased risk of challenges, some find no difference whatsoever and some find that children of single parents actually have more positive outcomes. It's easy to cherry-pick in this area without any consideration given to the detail of research, such as how much more of a risk is shown, or its limitations. As I described above, most of the studies that show negative outcomes are outdated, limited in their measures and conducted at a time when I really believe that social attitudes were driving research questions and interpretations. Others appear to deliberately overstate findings when there is really very little real-life difference. This is when I started to feel a bit uneasy about asking the question. I think a chapter like this is important because it can help reassure you, and is useful for showing others who might cling to outdated ideas that they can direct their concern elsewhere. But on the other hand, I started to feel as though we had to somehow justify that single parenting is okay. We don't.

So, having said all of that, let's have a quick look at the actual evidence. What does it say? Not a lot, to be honest, when you look at well-conducted studies from the last decade or so.

1. Differences are very small

One well-performed study that I found examined the health and wellbeing of 13,681 seven-year-olds from the Millennium Cohort study (a longitudinal study which started following children who were born in 2000–02).[2] It found some significant differences in outcomes for those children living in single-parent households or with their biological mother and father. However, those differences were small – incredibly small in places. For example, 0.4% of children living in two-parent households had poor health compared to 0.9% in single-parent households. Technically that's 'more than double' if you're a headline writer, but let's remember that 99% of children did not have poor health.

There were also small differences for other health measures. For weight, 7% of single-parent children were obese compared to 5% of those from two-parent families. For asthma 19% of single-parent children had a diagnosis compared to 14% of two-parent households. The study also looked at behaviour challenges, finding that 5% of those from two-parent families were considered to have high levels of difficulties, compared to 12% of those from single-parent households. These are just a few of the measures, but overall, most children were healthy, with a small increase in difficulties in single-parent families.

Any evidence of worse outcomes?

This is a good example of how sweeping statements about single parenting affecting health can be very overstated.

2. Poverty (which should be fixable) is the main issue

The previous study also examined the impact of poverty on health outcomes. Whereas 17% of those living in two-parent families were living in poverty, 62% of those in single-parent families were. The researchers re-ran the analyses considering the impact of poverty and found that there were no longer significant differences between single and two-parent families. Basically, it's differences in income that can affect health outcomes. Therefore, any discussion about the impact of single parenting should be about *a)* ensuring that the other parent financially supports their children, *b)* having increased financial support for situations such as bereavement and adoption, and *c)* enabling single parents to work more flexibly.

Indeed, I found one study that found very small differences in educational outcomes for children from single-parent families. However, these either disappeared or were reduced even further in countries that had more supportive social policies, such as family and child allowances and parental leave. Again, this shows me that any difference is nothing to do with being a single parent, and rather that single parents need more support.[3] We will return to this later in the financial support chapter.

3. Children of single parents by choice often have (slightly) better outcomes than those in two-parent homes

When we look at studies of single parenting (typically mothering) by choice, the results are overwhelmingly positive. This could be in part because parents have chosen this route, and although there may be challenges, other factors, such as a challenging co-parent, do not exist. Often, but not always, parents are protected by having a higher income than average, which has allowed them to consider single parenthood in the first place. Again, this highlights that if there were any differences in outcomes from single parenting, their root cause would not be the single parenting, but a wider, fixable context.

One study conducted in the 1990s compared outcomes for children born by IVF to either a single mother or a two-parent family. No differences in parent and teacher reported child behavioural or educational outcomes were found among children when they were seven years old. Interestingly, however, when parent conflict in two-parent homes was high, or parents had 'lower levels of love for each other', children were more likely to have behavioural problems. This is important when considering the suggestion that parents should stay together 'for the sake of the children'. If the relationship is not positive, what exactly is being modelled?[4]

Another study compared maternal anxiety and depression, adaptation to motherhood and maternal-infant bonding between single parents and women who were married who had IVF treatment. No significant differences were found.[5] Mothers were followed up when their children were two years old, and researchers found that the single mothers showed greater joy and lower levels of anger towards their children, and their children had fewer emotional and behavioural problems.[6]

Finally, a recent study compared 103 children who were conceived via IVF by single versus partnered parents.[7] The researchers took measures of maternal wellbeing and mother-child relationships, alongside child behaviour via child, parent and teacher report. To cut a long story short, again they found no differences in child behaviour or parenting quality, apart from lower levels of mother-child conflict for those in single-parent families. Notably the study examined the effect of financial difficulties on child emotional or behavioural difficulties, finding a small impact. It is the context that matters rather than solo parenting status – and again I will say that this context can likely be improved through better support structures for those parenting alone. Fix the context, rather than insisting on one type of family structure!

The biggest impact is on... maternal mental health

> *'It's lonely. The experiences are unique and lots of my friends were two-parent families, they just didn't understand the struggle.'* Martha

As with many aspects of parenting, when the newspaper headlines are screaming about irreparable harms to children, often it is not the children who are affected, but those who are doing the stellar job of loving and caring for them. The majority of studies in this area have been conducted with mothers (although some have emerged more recently with fathers). For example, one study found no impact of single parenting upon child mental health and development, but the mothers were more likely to have high symptoms of depression.[8] Another study found that over a quarter of single mothers had clinically significant levels of depression, compared to around one in six partnered mothers. Notably, depression score was linked to financial pressures, challenging ex-partner relationships and a lack of social support. Again, it's the broader experience of single parenting and a lack of support that predicts wellbeing rather than the core experience of family set-up.[9]

For example, not being able to afford to feed your child can feel overwhelmingly stressful, especially in the current cost-of-living crisis. In one study with 22 single mothers many talked about having to make careful meal and food plans, and shopping around to try to make money go further. There was often a need to focus on foods that their children would *a)* eat and not waste and *b)* that filled them up, rather than on nutritional content. Many had to make a concerted effort not to react angrily if food was dropped on the floor or a child suddenly decided they weren't hungry or didn't like a food they had previously. This left many mothers feeling guilty, stressed and frustrated.[10] Other studies have highlighted how often mothers skipped meals themselves to make sure their children were fed, leaving them feeling run-down and exhausted.[11]

Another significant trigger for mental health difficulties is an abusive relationship with an ex-partner, particularly if you are attempting to co-parent with someone who is difficult or acts poorly. In one study with 59 younger single mothers, 4 out of 10 had experienced an abusive relationship in the last year. Over half had significant symptoms of depression.[12] Another study highlighted how often financial difficulties or fear of losing any support whatsoever meant that some single mothers deliberately kept in contact with an abusive co-parent because of fears that they would not survive alone.[13]

The experience of an abusive relationship can leave women blaming themselves, losing confidence and living in fear. Of course, the blame should be firmly on the abuser, but social stereotypes often mean that women are blamed for the behaviour of men, ignoring their strength in continuing to support their children. Abuse may be physical or financial, and childcare contact arrangements are often used to continue to abuse women in other ways, leaving them worried about whether maintenance will be paid, an abusive co-parent will keep to childcare arrangements, or whether the co-parent will emotionally harm their child. Stalking is common, through social media or through directly asking children questions, with that information then used to exert control. Court orders, the 'right' to see children and financial imbalances fuel this situation.

On top of this, women are often gaslit into downplaying concerns or believing that a father-child relationship is more important than all other issues. In one study women talked about how people would tell them that it was important for their children to maintain a relationship with their father, or dismiss abusive behaviours, as the father child relationship mattered more.[14] Men often deliberately appeared charming and attentive in front of others, often showering children with gifts (in contrast to a mother financially struggling from day-to-day). When mothers tried to talk about the private and controlling abuse they experienced, they were dismissed by people close to them. Is it any wonder, with the combination of abuse, control, and gaslighting, that women end up depressed and anxious?

There has been much less research into single fathers and mental health. One study explored the differential impact upon mental health for single mothers and fathers. It found that single parents tended to have increased rates of high psychological distress compared to coupled parents, but that single mothers had a higher rate (16%) compared to single fathers (9%). The authors hypothesised that greater financial security among men explained this difference.[15] However, other studies have also pointed to more positive social reactions towards single fathers, with lower levels of criticism and higher levels of almost 'awe' at the role they are playing. Understandably over time this is likely to impact upon wellbeing.[16]

In Part II we will explore some of the specific challenges of single parenting, and some suggested solutions.

PART II
EXPLORING SOME OF THE CHALLENGES OF SINGLE PARENTING

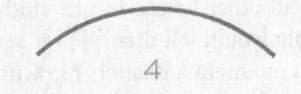

4
Supporting your child through change

> *'My main concerns are around how the kids will be affected by his terrible parenting as he has mostly disappeared but pops up every now and again to mess with their heads. I try to protect them from it as best I can, but ultimately there will always be a father-shaped hole in their hearts, and I must accept that. But it's massively easier without him.'* Becky

Although in the previous chapters I have shown that negative stereotypes about the outcomes of single parenting are simply untrue, it is nonetheless the case that experiences in the context of single parenting can be some of the most difficult times in your and your children's life. Although some parents will separate amicably, even the process of separating out lives and starting to build a new one can feel overwhelming. For

Supporting your child through change

those who make the decision to go it alone by choice, even when you are ready the decision can bring about all sorts of anxieties. And then of course we have parents who would never want to be in this situation, who separate due to the traumas of abuse or adultery, or are bereaved. It's important that we recognise the impact of these changes on children and highlight the support that is needed, without getting caught up in judgemental headlines and beliefs.

What can make separation, loss or a decision to go it alone feel so enormous is worrying about how your child or children will feel and cope. You're battling your own feelings too and may want to simply crawl into bed until it all goes away. But you can't. You have to parent and more than that, while trying to control your own feelings you are trying to support your children with theirs and behave in a way that helps them to process it. You might be angry – at your former partner, the unfairness of infertility or at the universe for taking your partner away from you. You try to juggle, worrying that you're not doing it right, despite a very real need to support your own wellbeing. As Hayley describes:

'In the early days after my husband died, I was shell-shocked, but had to carry on, getting back to uni classes a few weeks after he died. I didn't have time to really grieve until I returned to the UK the following year but remember crying in the car on the way to university most days after I'd dropped my daughter at childcare. I felt like I wasn't a good mum during this time and feel a lot of shame looking back. I was incredibly angry for a long time. I missed my husband, I missed the life we might have had, I was angry that my daughter had lost her dad, that I may well not have another child, exhausted by the sheer grind of parenting alone'.

Why Single Parents Matter

The challenges that you experience will differ according to your situation. However, having said that, underlying many separations, loss, and decisions to go it alone are likely to be the core emotions of anxiety, anger and questions about their other parent/s. This chapter is going to explore some of the ways you can support your children, with ideas from our single-parent contributors. There are some further ideas, specifically around new relationships, co-parenting and finances, in the coming chapters. A short book can't cover everything, but the charity Gingerbread also has lots of excellent information and support for the experience of single parenting in general, as well as an excellent list of ideas to support your child. See www.gingerbread.org.uk/find-information/managing-separation/helping-children-through-separation

Here is some guidance from our parent contributors:

1. Reassure them that most of all they are loved

'Reassure them that they are loved and that it's not their fault.' Martha

This is probably the number one piece of advice in this. Helping children feel loved, wanted, and secure is key to attachment, self-esteem and wellbeing. The good news is that research has shown that even when children are let down by numerous other people around them, if they have an established, secure relationship with just one person, they can continue to thrive. If they're adopted or conceived through solo IVF they'll likely have questions – but questions aren't bad. If they lose their other parent through bad behaviour or bereavement, they may struggle with that. A common worry is feeling that you have to make up for loss or absence, as in Becky's words at the start of the chapter. But *you are enough*. These things don't mean that they don't feel loved and cared

Supporting your child through change

for by *you*. They will thrive, in spite of everything, because they know they are loved.

2. Encourage them to talk about how they feel (and listen to them)

'Encourage them to talk about it. Ask a trusted family member who can be reasonably neutral to talk to them about it separately and give them an opportunity to talk away from you. Children will worry about the impact on you and will hide things. Encourage them to be honest with you and try not to put your own feelings into the response. Listen to them and show you believe them and take their concerns seriously.' Jennie

Not all children will react in the same way to separation or loss. Some may feel anxious, angry or sad, while others seemingly bounce through it. There is no right way for a child to react; i.e. if your child is angry, or alternatively doesn't seem bothered, then that is what is right for them at the time. They may feel differently later on. What is important is helping them to label those feelings, understand them and for you to validate them. Younger children might need help identifying their emotions. Talking to them about book characters that feel angry or sad can help. You could ask them to draw pictures of how they are feeling if words are difficult. For older children, instant messaging or talking in the car when everyone can look straight ahead can help get those difficult feelings out.

Children and teens might also play out their emotions in different ways. Younger children might 'regress', acting much younger than they are or taking a step back with things like sleep or toilet training. Reassure them, and talk about what will happen day to day. Older children might become more rebellious or angry at you. Consistency, calmness and reminding them (and showing them) that they are loved and cared for helps. The charity Relate has a great list of ways to support different emotions in your child: planner.relate.org.uk/children/talking-your-children/understanding-your-childs-needs-and-behaviour

If your child is struggling with how they feel there are different options for therapy to help support them, including play therapy and organisations that specifically focus on grief and talking. You might like to talk to your child about how you deal with difficult emotions, for example by saying that when you're feeling angry you like to go for a walk, or if you're feeling sad you like to curl up with a good book and your blanket. Have a look at the Resources section at the back of the book for details of where to get support with this.

3. Reach out to others to help you support them

'Other bereaved parents have found Winston's Wish to be a real help for their children, but when I tried to get help for my daughter I was told she was too young (she was 4 or 5 at the time). However, her school were able to provide some art therapy for her which was great at helping her navigate the anger and strong emotions she felt (and still feels) about her dad's death'. Hayley

Although you might feel very alone, you are not and there are people and organisations that can help you and your child. Telling school, childcare or any clubs about the situation can help them understand and support your child. There are also a number of charities which can help you through all sorts of aspects of separation, loss and a decision to go it alone. Have a look at the useful organisations at the back of the book.

Supporting your child through change

4. Give them age-appropriate factual information

'There's a lot of advice saying that you shouldn't run the other parent down in front of the kids. I agree with this to a point, but in my case I felt it important to be age-appropriately honest with my children about their father's behaviour. It's important to me that they know he is the one with the problem and not them. Children can be left feeling unworthy when their parent doesn't love them as they should. I want my kids to know it's not about them. I want them to know they're amazing and that they deserve better. So I don't call their father names or anything like that, but we do talk about how what Dad is doing is not okay, not about them – we talk about why Dad is like that. I don't instigate the conversations, but I am honest with them if they ask me.' Becky

We often think that if we don't tell children what is going on then we are protecting them from it. But children generally cope better when they know the truth and what to expect. If the truth is hidden from them they will pick up on it, and likely create their own anxieties and worry about why they aren't being told the truth. Not telling them about things doesn't make the situation go away and risks them blaming themselves. Beliefs such as 'Daddy left because I didn't keep my room tidy' are common. This is why simple information about why a separation has occurred, and reassurance that it is not their fault, can help them process it.

However, balancing giving facts with emotional reactions is an art form here. A younger child, for example, might need to know that mummy and daddy are not going to live together anymore because they will be happier living in separate homes. You could say, 'You will still see us both and have a bedroom at each house with all your things'. They don't need to know the details of an affair or your honest description of your partner's behaviour – save that for your friends.

It might help, if you know in advance that a separation is on the cards, to think about a list of potential questions your child might ask and how you are going to respond to them. How much detail will you share? Knowing when they are ready to hear more of the truth about the breakdown of your relationship is an individual thing. Follow their lead to some extent. You might find that younger children seem oblivious, seeing only the positives. As they get older and start to question things, you might want to start giving them more specific, factual details. Try to leave the emotion or blame out of it, a little like people tell you to speak to a partner or child about their behaviour: call out the behaviour not the person. There is a huge difference between 'Daddy made me very upset' and 'Daddy is an awful person'.

Likewise, recognising children's emotions if they are being let down or treated poorly is important. As Becky describes above, when a co-parent is absent, distant or not supportive this can make children worry that it's their fault and something about their behaviour. Recognising their emotions, validating them and explaining how it is poor behaviour on the part of their other parent can really help. Remember that your child will likely have a lot of emotions going on regarding their relationship with their other parent, so a bit like when your friend breaks up with her terrible boyfriend yet again, try not to criticise them directly. As above, acknowledge how your children feel, how upsetting it is, and how it's not their fault. Try not to call the other parent a [insert insult of choice here]! If children think that you want them to dislike or hate the other parent, they might feel guilty about having any positive feelings about them or still wanting to see them. There is more on dealing with your child's reaction to a difficult co-parent in the next chapter.

Supporting your child through change

CAFCASS (Children and Family Court Advisory and Support Service) have two excellent leaflets entitled 'My family is changing' – one for younger children and one for teens – to help with these conversations. You can download them here: www.cafcass.gov.uk/young-people/resources-young-people

5. Try to keep a friendly and united appearance with their other parent

   'We were advised to tell the children that we were separating together, to reassure them that we would still both be in their lives and what would happen. We did this but it was one of the hardest things I have ever done. There were some difficult years after the split but I did my best to be friendly and light around him if the children were there. I think it helped them feel less anxious and more reassured… at least I hope it did because it was excruciating at times for me to put my hurt and anger aside.' Rebecca

As Rebecca explains, this is possibly one of the hardest parts of a separation. As above, your children will likely have complex emotions around their other parent and how much they want to see them. If they think that you are angry at the other parent or very upset when they leave to go and spend time with them, this can make them feel really conflicted about wanting to go. If possible, try to have a united co-parenting relationship (more on this in Chapter 5). Little things like keeping to routines, and trying where possible to have similar rules about things like screen time and snacks in each house, can help your children know what the rules and boundaries are, which helps them feel secure. Also, try not to let your children overhear you ranting about your ex-partner. Doing so can feel therapeutic, but check that little ears aren't listening or do it by instant messaging (which also allows on point gifs to be added).

6. Support their relationship with others

'For me ensuring she still has a relationship with her father's extended family has been important, though it hasn't been easy.' Elizabeth

This is another tricky one for you. I do realise I'm saying almost all points are tricky, but I think this shows just how overwhelming supporting your child can be. If your ex-partner is still active in your child's life, then they will likely enable this. If they are not, or they have passed away, then helping your child maintain a relationship with that side of their family might be important. I say might, because you know your child and their extended family best. If they are ultimately supportive and caring then helping them maintain that connection through emails, visits, video calls and so on can help your child understand that part of their identity and give them the feeling of being part of a wider family.

7. Support them to talk about happy memories

'I often show my daughter photos around her early life including photos of both Sarah and I. We're smiling and having fun in many of these and I think although it can bring up lots of difficult emotions for me, it's important that she sees those. I want her to know that we wanted her and she was loved.' Lauren

Yeah, I know. It's tricky again. Showing photos and talking about memories, no matter how difficult, helps to show children that they did come from a place of love. Acknowledging that happy times did occur, and letting your children show joy about them, can help them feel at ease and connected to their other parent and feelings about family.

Supporting your child through change

> '*Make sure they have access to photos of birth parents and foster carers and that they can ask anything, to get your child involved in letterbox, e.g. draw a picture for them, are there questions they want to know, e.g. what is birth mummy's favourite food.*' <u>Karyn</u>

For parents who are bereaved or who are single adopters this might be different again – with its own set of emotions and tricky questions. Support their questions, be honest when you don't know, and help them to build a box of memories.

8. Remember you know your child best

> '*Go with your gut instinct first. You know your own children better than any therapist ever will. It's good to go and see someone to get tips and support for other ways to help them but at the end of the day you are the one with them when they ask pertinent questions. Theory of guidance and books is that a lot of the time. It's theory. How it plays out in practice has much nuance and for good reason. Because each child responds differently and that changes with age too.*' <u>Pete</u>

Finally, as always, remember that you know your child best. There is so much advice out there on supporting children through separation, loss or finding out about their adoption or conception. Not everything will apply to your child. Not all relationships should be encouraged. Not every child needs therapy and some might hate it. Follow your child's lead, keep talking and most of all, keep loving them.

5

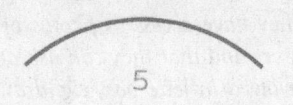

Co-parenting

This chapter explores some of the challenges of co-parenting or sharing care of your child with their other parent. As with the rest of this book, there are no right or wrong answers and how you decide to share (or end up sharing) care if your child's other parent is around will depend on lots of things including your child's age, their relationship with their other parent, and practicalities.

I also want to acknowledge openly here the frustrations, anger and grief at not having a co-parent to parent with. Some parents will have abandoned their children, some will have died, and some will not be part of their lives due to adoption or solo IVF. It can be incredibly hard to know that you do not have any sort of co-parent to share any of the load with. Hearing others complain can feel insensitive and it can exacerbate feelings of loss around abandonment, abuse, bereavement, and infertility. I have no magic solution, although I suggest you try to surround yourself with supportive friends and take every offer of help and kindness possible, but I want to acknowledge the very

Co-parenting

real and difficult feelings here. If you're in this situation you might want to skip to the next chapter.

How much should we share care?

'Make the decision that is best for the child at that time. My eldest used to be really impacted when we first trialled one week on one week off shared care, so I put a stop to it. It was not benefiting the child. I called the shots as the main carer.' Nicole

One of the most pressing questions is often 'how often should my child see their other parent?'. As above, any legal expert will tell you that this decision must be made in the best interests of the child and any psychologist would say that you should look to your child, what they want and need and think about what works best for them. However, your wellbeing and financial health are also considerations, as these are intertwined with your child's interests. There are several ways in which you can agree on how much you will each see your child. This includes you coming to an agreement together, professional mediation to help you reach a decision, and going to court when you cannot agree.

In most cases children benefit from consistent and regular contact with their other parent and any court would want to maintain that unless there is a danger to the child. Let's work on the basis for the moment that you have a good co-parenting relationship with your ex-partner and that they are in a stable position to be able to care for your child well and they want to do so (more details later on what to do if you are not in this situation). Some of the main things that you need to think about are continuity, stability and routine for your child. Children are generally happiest when they know what is going to happen. Some struggle with change more than others.

Some parents do choose to share care equally, perhaps splitting each week or alternating one week at each house. However, many choose a pattern of every other weekend, often with one night in the week. This gives a balance of time with the other parent, but also a stable routine where children spend most of the time in one place. Unfortunately, this does place the brunt of the caring responsibility on one parent, but equally if you are the main caregiver you might want that to happen. It's fine to have very mixed emotions around this.

Some things you might like to think about include:

- *Age of children.* More on this a little later, but if you have a baby or toddler who is used to being with one parent (in most cases their mother) then maintaining this connection will be important. This will be especially important if a baby or child is breastfed. Any overnight (or indeed shorter) separations may impact upon feeding.
- *Previous care status quo.* Stability is important, especially for younger children. If you previously equally shared the day-to-day care for your child (including the emotional load of thinking about what needed to be done!), then an arrangement in which care is shared more equally may work. If you were in a set-up in which one parent stayed at home, or did the majority of pick-ups and day-to-day care, then your child may find it more reassuring if this continues, at least initially. It might be that you separate before your baby is born (or soon after) and this will require different arrangements again (see the section below 'What if one of your children is a baby').
- *Location of school, clubs and friends.* If you live close to each other this is far less of an issue, but if one parent

Co-parenting

has moved even a small distance away then this can make things trickier on a day-to-day basis in terms of getting to school, or when children are older and they want to hang out with friends after school and on weekends.

- *Space in homes.* I do not mean that you need to have a castle to have your child stay with you, but living circumstances do need to be taken into account. Sometimes a parent will not yet have a permanent home to live in and might be staying with relatives or in a temporary smaller place. In these situations, sometimes parents choose to see their children every weekend, but not overnight.
- *How well your child adapts to transitions.* Some children happily bounce between homes at ease. Others feel a bit unsettled for the first few hours or night after a 'move' (or leading up to it). If your child seems unsettled, you might find that a block of nights works better.
- *Working patterns.* Some jobs have more flexibility or standardised hours than others. In an ideal world you will want to support the other parent to continue working, as this will provide financial security for your child. This is not the same as them using work as an excuse to get out of parenting, but a case of maintaining stability for your child.
- *Any additional needs that your child might have.* This might include a physical disability and a need to be in a place that has any adaptations or specialist equipment they might need. Children who are autistic may also have preferences for routine, places they are familiar with and as little change as possible.
- *How well your child knows the other parent and how they feel about staying with them.* It may be that a younger

child feels nervous and needs more time and flexibility to adapt. As children get older, they may be more likely to voice an opinion, especially if they do not feel so welcome in their other home. Listen to their concerns, but try to support a continued relationship with their other parent when possible. A child admitting they don't want to go because they've got a better games console at home is different to a child feeling uncomfortable or that they're not being cared for.

Remember that what you choose to do at the start does not need to be set in stone forever. Although it might be more practical and easier, you also do not necessarily have to have the same pattern of contact for every child. For example, if you have an older teen they may be more reluctant to move between homes, or if you have a younger baby they might spend less time away from their mother (see below). You might prefer to keep things flexible, allowing children to spend more or less time with their other parent as they get older. This decision needs to be taken with some consideration of practicalities i.e. distance, or need to work. Remember you are also allowed to factor in your own wellbeing, i.e. needing some time alone or wanting the other parent to take a responsible role.

One idea that you could use is to draw up a parenting plan or shared diary (perhaps using a document or a specific planner) for your child. I'm reminded of the 'my day' diaries that my children used to have in childcare that said what they'd done, eaten etc. You could leave each other notes in the diary if you don't feel comfortable sending direct messages. It could also include important information such as appointments, illnesses, medication or dietary needs. You could also draw up a list of agreed rules for caring for your child, such as around screentime or diet, but this would need to be considered flexibly. Involve your co-parent in decisions if possible. Unfortunately, you cannot control what the other parent chooses to do with or feed your child unless there are serious concerns.

CAFCASS has a great document here on things you might like to consider: www.helpguide.org/articles/parenting-family/co-parenting-tips-for-divorced-parents.htm

Supporting your child through their time away from you

All children are different. Some will bounce off happily to stay with their other parent without a single backward glance in your direction. Others will find the transition more difficult, either due to differences between your home environments or from not having contact with you. Potential solutions might depend on the age of your child (and to some extent sadly the co-operation of their other parent). Some things you can try:

- Letting them take comfort items with them to their other house. Young children might like to take something that reminds them of you, such as an item of clothing.
- If possible, making sure both houses feel like home. Setting up their bedroom with familiar items, or indeed having novel items at each house to look forward to.
- Having a calendar that your child can see to know when they will be going and coming back. Some children like there to be firm plans when they are away, i.e. you will go and see Granny on Saturday and on Sunday you'll go swimming.
- Set times to contact you, or for older children, a mobile phone that they can send you messages on. However, some children are more settled if they don't contact you. Follow your child's lead.

- Some of the techniques used when children are nervous being separated from you in settings such as school or childcare. Drawing matching hearts on your hands and talking about how they are connected. Looking out for shared things such as the sun or moon in the sky – again for shared connection.
- Keep to routines as much as possible, such as school drop-off times and clubs. Supporting friendships at both homes.
- Be as positive as possible about your child seeing their other parent (as long as there are no real concerns) so they don't feel anxious about upsetting you. Try to be positive and happy about the good experiences they have with the other parent (to your child at least – offload to a friend later!).
- Let your children talk about how they feel. The charity Action for Children suggests encouraging children to write down their feelings in a notebook, or to write them down and place them away in a 'worry box'. Younger children could draw a 'worry monster' eating their worries: parents.actionforchildren.org.uk/parenting-relationships/separation-divorce/worried-about-contact
- If you can, speak to your co-parent about how your child feels so they can also reinforce positive feelings.

Remember through all of this that you matter too. Of course, your focus will be on supporting your child and trying to maintain a happy façade, at least as they leave, but it's okay for you to need support as well. Sometimes it can feel like a break, at other times like your heart is being ripped out, especially if you carry difficult memories or trauma from your relationship. This may get easier, or it may not. Certain days, like your first Christmas or birthday apart, can make you feel lost and unsettled in the run-up and it can be hard to work out why until you realise. I could say stay busy and do stuff you don't get to do when caring for your child, but that's not going to help if the feelings are too big. Be kind to yourself: don't put pressure on yourself to get on with things. Alternatively, you could distract yourself by at least having free access to tidy their rooms! Remember time does pass. Getting out of the house often helps. Lean on people. Start a coming home ritual. Create new celebrations and days. Have a separate birthday celebration on their due date, almost birthday or have two celebrations like the King. There's always room for more cake.

What if one of your children is a baby?

Sharing care for children who are preschool age and above and have already formed a relationship with both parents is different to sharing care if a younger baby is involved. Babies have very different needs to older children, and this may affect what a shared parenting arrangement will look like at the start. It is perfectly okay to have a different shared-care relationship for older children compared to a baby.

From a biological norm perspective babies are typically predominantly cared for by their mother during the early months while also developing a relationship with their father or other parent. This gradually changes as babies get older. The World Health Organization recommends that babies are breastfed for up to two years and beyond. Although there will of course be variations on this balance between parents, supporting existing bonds (and breastfeeding if relevant) to continue, if possible, will most likely be in the best interests of your baby. Any shared parenting arrangement should respect this while also allowing a relationship with the father/other parent to continue. If it is taken to court a judge *should* support this, and there is plenty of evidence to back up your argument. So what might shared care look like with a baby?

Writing this from the perspective of the mother, if you are separated from your child's other parent from before birth or in the early weeks a typical pattern might be for regular short visits, usually with you present or even in your home if that is okay with you. Contact is important to build a bond, but it should not be at the expense of a baby who needs to form a core attachment relationship with you. This can change slowly over time. As your baby grows their other parent may take them out for a few hours and then for the day. You could work towards overnights by the end of the first year or so, depending on whether your child is breastfeeding and how comfortable they feel being cared for by their other parent. Distance will matter here. There is a difference between your child staying overnight locally and a longer journey that is not easy to return from. Of course timeframes are flexible and you might feel more comfortable sooner, or not until later.

If you do have a good relationship with your co-parent, some former couples might consider having an overnight at each other's house – in a separate bedroom – so that the baby has contact with the other parent but is not away from their mother. This also helps if your baby is breastfed. Of course, this is going to depend hugely on the relationship you have and the circumstances around you not being together. It might also be confusing if older children are involved. Your feelings matter here and should not be brushed aside 'just to make things easier'. This arrangement probably won't work for many, but I wanted to give it as an option.

If you are breastfeeding, there should never be any pressure for breastfeeding to stop simply to allow overnight or extended care. It is important to maintain breastfeeding because we know that it protects both child and maternal health. Some babies will take expressed milk in a bottle more readily than others, but it's also important to remember that it's not just about food. Breastfeeding is also a form of connection and reassurance for babies and children, and this is especially important during stressful times. Premature weaning can be particularly difficult for older children and is something to gently manage when the time is right for mother and child, rather than being forced unnecessarily, especially during times of change. We also know that women's experiences of having to stop breastfeeding before they are ready can lead to grief, anger and guilt and ultimately be very long-lasting. It is possible that if your child is older your co-parent may ask for more time with them, and you should consider how that might be facilitated, but a co-parent cannot insist that breastfeeding stops. La Leche League Great Britain has a great info sheet with more suggestions on how to manage this: www.laleche.org.uk/breastfeeding-contact-cases. I also recommend Emma Pickett's book *Supporting Breastfeeding Past the First Six Months and Beyond* for help with any challenges feeding older babies and children.

What if my child's other parent struggles to provide a safe living/meeting space?

If your child's other parent has nowhere safe to take your children or is experiencing difficulties that mean they may not be fully safe in their care, there is an option to maintain a relationship through child contact centres. This may be something that is dictated by social services or a court if they are worried about the safety of your child, or you might explore it on your own. The National Association of Child Contact Centres (NACCC) is a registered charity which has set up a network of child contact centres. These are neutral places where children of separated families can spend time with non-resident parents and sometimes other family members, in a comfortable and safe environment. Alongside providing a safe and fun meeting place they also help support parents to develop parenting skills, promote mediation to strengthen relationships and can help with specialist interventions when situations are more complex. You can find out more about them here: naccc.org.uk

What if your co-parenting relationship is difficult?

'The relationship has been pretty damaging. On and off contact with no respect for my rules and boundaries. Children were re-dressed when arriving at his house into 'their' clothes. They were not allowed to bring toys from Dad's house to my house. Negative things were said about me in front of them. They are very positive now about my parenting and very negative about Dad's'. Evangeline

The suggestions for contact above rely on some level of respectful communication and good behaviour between yourself and your child's other parent. If you are unable to agree on a contact schedule, or are worried about your child not being safe in their co-parent's care, you have the option to participate in mediation, and then if that doesn't work, formalising arrangements through a court. This is time-consuming, costly (although financial support is available) and stressful, but in some cases trying to continue to communicate and agree on a solution is more so. If your partner is being threatening during discussions you can seek advice directly from Citizen's Advice, or from an organisation such as Women's Aid or the Men's Advice line.

Courts typically require you to have tried mediation first before you take a case to court. Professional mediation allows you to discuss contact arrangements with your child's other

Co-parenting

parent with the support of a trained mediator. You might be in the room together, or you might start in separate rooms if it is too difficult. Some places also now offer it online. A mediator will not tell you what to do, but will try to facilitate a discussion that is in your child's best interests. Legal aid is sometimes available if you cannot afford it. Mediation has a success rate of around 70%, but in some cases it will not work. You can find out more, including about what to expect, on the Family Mediation Council website www.familymediationcouncil.org.uk/family-mediation

Sometimes mediation does not work, and you need to attend court to finalise the childcare and support relationships for your children. This is known as a child arrangement order and considers who the child will live with, who will have contact with the child, and how often and for how long that contact should be. It could be that you want your child's other parent to see more or less of them (or they are asking for more contact). Courts will only make a child arrangement order if they believe it is in the best interests of your child, and they should not force a child to spend time (or lengthy time) with a parent who is not acting in their best interests. Likewise, a parent can ask for an arrangement if they feel that they are not able to see their child as frequently as they want to due to the malevolent actions of the other parent. Before you attend court, you will be allocated a CAFCASS officer. They will work with your family to assess any risks to the children and consider whether a decision can be made through mediation.

Any decision will be made in the best interests of the child. The NSPCC states that courts will consider the following:

- The wishes and feelings of the child
- Any harm or risk of harm
- The child's physical, emotional, and educational needs

- The likely effect of any change in the child's circumstances
- The child's age, sex, background, and characteristics
- The ability of each parent to meet the child's needs

Once a contact arrangement is in place it should be followed. A parent can only refuse to see their child if they believe their child will come to harm in their care. However, to uphold this you would need to contact the court to show that the parent has breached the order. Understandably, many parents do not do this due to the time and stress involved, meaning that although the arrangement is legally binding, some parents wriggle out of the responsibility, knowing the other parent will not report them. More details on what to do if your child refuses to see their other parent are given below.

Strategies for communicating with a difficult co-parent

> *'Keep it practical and concise, cut out the emotional response and save that for chats with your mates for support.'* Jess

Relationship breakdown can naturally result in tense communication when you need to remain in regular contact to co-parent your children. Unless your split has been amicable there will likely be a difficult history, from broken promises to abusive behaviour. Whereas in previous relationships you may have had the option of ceasing all contact to help yourself heal from the relationship and move on, the cruel twist of separating from your child's other parent is that you often need to remain in each other's lives. It's harder to pretend you don't know them.

In Chapter 3 we talked about the impact of difficult co-

Co-parenting

parenting relationships on mental health in relation to 'outcomes' of single parenting. Unfortunately, some ex-partners will use their children to try to maintain control over you. They can be difficult around contact arrangements, use the need to contact you as an avenue to criticise or abuse you, and participate in financial abuse (more on this in the next chapter). Court orders and discussions around the 'rights of the father' have led some ex-partners to abuse this legislation, which was set up to protect children, to continue to control and abuse their former partner.

You might also experience the absent co-parent, or one who plays a minimal, ad hoc role in your children's lives. This parent fails to turn up for contact or does whatever they can to get out of it, goes away on holiday a lot (but never takes your children) and tries to wriggle out of any financial support. Aside from feeling deeply frustrating and unfair, it can leave you on edge wondering if they will turn up, whether you'll be able to afford things and generally exhausted.

If you are finding that your child's other parent is difficult to communicate with, there are a number of strategies that might help.

- Ask for communication to be in writing, maybe via a specific email address so you can check at a regular time suitable for you. This also means that you have any communication in writing. Alternatively set up a different ring/text tone alert for them so you don't jump every time you get a notification.
- Try to communicate calmly and don't put any rants or threats in writing. Text as if your messages could be read out in court – calmly and politely. What you mutter while writing them is up to you.
- Just because the other person's behaviour is unfair,

doesn't mean you should fight fire with fire. If they are manipulative and controlling and you react this could be used against you.
- The idea above of keeping a diary between you in which you record useful information about your baby/child and their care can save you having long conversations but keeps you both updated and helps you share things you'd like the other parent to do.
- Meet on neutral ground for handovers so they do not need to come to your house.
- Try to stick to a regular pattern of contact so you don't have to keep making arrangements.
- Try to remain calm in front of your child and not to complain about the other parent in front of them. When children feel that their separated parents have a civil relationship, they feel more secure. Yes, this does take intense gritting of teeth. When they get older you might slowly start to change this (see below). Again, lean on friends and family and consider counselling if you're really struggling.
- Choose your battles. Your ex is going to really frustrate you at times (remember that's probably why they're an ex). But try and let the little things go. Don't let them goad you. Focus on the important stuff. This is a great skill to practise for when your child is a teenager.
- Try to make sure you have someone to talk to about the stress of shared care with a difficult co-parent. Having to hand your child over to someone who has been emotionally or physically abusive towards you, even if they show kindness and care to your child, can be one of the hardest things you ever have to do (and is a further reason why 'oh you're so lucky to have a break' can feel so incredibly insensitive).

Co-parenting

- Finally, if you are worried about your child's safety or your ex-partner is making threats towards you, you can contact CAFCASS for advice on whether a court could be involved in reducing contact or preventing them from coming near your home. See www.cafcass.gov.uk/grown-ups/parents-and-carers/divorce-and-separation/harmful-conflict

What if your child's other parent doesn't want contact?

'His father had contact with him in the early years after the divorce, but this dwindled over time. This was mostly due to his father not having an active interest in parenting and as a result my son was less and less keen to see him. In the last three years there has been essentially no contact bar an occasional text or phone call. I have only had direct contact with him once in the last three years. He does not pay maintenance and only did for a couple of months when my son was six. He has never shared any of the emotional or practical load of parenting. My son just shrugs when his father is mentioned and never spontaneously talks about him. He does not wish to contact him even though I make sure he can if he wants to. But I feel very proud to have raised him with very little support. We have a close relationship and he's grown into a fantastic young man.' Jess

If your child's other parent doesn't want contact or regularly fails to turn up when agreed, you could decide to ask the courts to put an order in place for them to see them. However, the court will most likely act in the best wishes of your child. If the other parent refuses to see your child, treats them poorly and is generally not caring for them well, a court is unlikely to formally assign care to them. Or in other words, if you're in a situation in which you need to take the other parent to court to make them see their child, it's unlikely to be granted. The other parent will, however, carry more financial responsibility for your child.

As Jess says above, children often pick up on their parent's reluctance or lack of effort to see them and don't desire to be part of that anymore. This can feel very tough on you, as you are carrying the weight of the childcare as well as supporting your child, often also taking on the financial load if the other parent dodges paying maintenance. Focus on the bond you have with your child and take pride in what you have done, and the reward of knowing what a strong bond you are forming.

Supporting your child when their other parent treats them badly

'His father had contact until about 18 months ago. He was always reluctant to follow our schedule and continued to use our son as a tool for control and manipulation. In the end he told our son (then aged five) that he no longer wished to see him. He then backtracked a few weeks later, threatening to take me to mediation or to court, but nothing transpired. He's made no real effort to remain in contact with our son, who has had therapy to help him process his big feelings around this experience. Our son occasionally talks about his dad, but never expresses any real desire to see him. It's also been made clear to me that he is telling people I am keeping our son from him, that I stopped and prevent contact, and that there's nothing he can do to engage in contact with our son despite knowing where we live. He has now missed two consecutive birthdays and Christmases.' Martha

What do you do if your child's other parent treats them badly?

Perhaps they are not reliable when it comes to seeing them, or maybe they have disappeared altogether. The previous chapter on supporting your child has a lot of ideas, but I want to come back to the idea of simply loving your child, reassuring them and talking about how it isn't their fault.

In terms of talking to your child and reassuring them, there is a fine balance between not using your child as a sounding board when you are frustrated with the other parent and not leaving them feeling confused if you appear supportive when the other parent is behaving badly. You will be the best judge of what your child can understand. Of course, this depends on how 'badly' the parent is behaving. Anything involving physical abuse, neglect or a lack of safety is different to a parent letting them down at the last minute or failing to be involved in their lives.

A co-parent may generally let your child down – i.e. picking them up late or not at all, not being very involved with them when they are caring for them, or simply not showing much of an interest in their lives. When children are younger you might start with simply acknowledging their emotions when something happens. A simple 'it feels sad when daddy doesn't pick you up, doesn't it' or 'that feels disappointing' can help them to manage their emotions. It doesn't blame the other parent but acknowledges your child's feelings, helps them to identify them and helps them feel like they are not feeling the 'wrong' thing.

'As they got older and they asked questions I would be honest with them as much as they needed to hear for their age.' Nicole

As children get older, particularly when they are teens, you might start to give more age-appropriate information, labelling behaviours as unsupportive or disappointing. Again, it's important that you still try not to directly criticise the other parent, but rather their behaviour, acknowledging calmly how it makes you feel. At this age children are more likely to share feelings about being disappointed, or hint at these thoughts, testing you out. Younger children often don't see poor behaviour or idolise their parent for the bare minimum. As they become more aware (and especially in the teenage years) they may slowly realise the differences and see where they have not been treated as well as they should. If you've put up with this for years it's difficult not to have a moment where you smile at justice, even though your heart is breaking for your child's anger and loss. You may feel guilty that you didn't try hard enough, or feel empty at the loss of that trust between your child and their other parent. Again, honesty, listening to emotions and reminding your child that they've done nothing wrong, and this isn't their fault or responsibility, can help. Follow their lead in how much information you slowly give them.

If your child starts not to want to see their other parent because of their behaviour, try to talk to them calmly about why. What is happening and how do they feel? On the one hand a co-parent seeing their child should be encouraged, but when does their behaviour warrant you supporting your child *not* to see them? If your child really does not want to see their other parent because they feel too upset by it, you could try to talk to the other parent. Is it something they could easily change to make your child feel more accepted and comfortable (favourite toys, foods, trips out, enabling friendships)? Try to phrase this calmly and neutrally if possible, rather than blaming the other parent.

If it is something more fundamentally harmful, such as abusive or neglectful behaviour, or overhearing a lot of

Co-parenting

arguments or a lot of criticism of you, which is making your child not want to see their other parent, you could make the decision for your child to remain with you for their own safety. However, it is important to know that the other parent does have the right to see their child, unless this is prevented by a court. Often parents who are neglectful or unsupportive of their children let go of contact fairly easily, but some may use it as a way to try to control you all. Seeking support from CAFCASS or an organisation such as Gingerbread can help you to legally but safely work out a plan.

The question of whether or not your child can refuse to see their other parent is a bit complicated. The NSPCC website states 'A child can't be forced to see the non-resident parent but if there's a court order in place, the resident parent must follow the agreed arrangements'. This essentially means that you should both facilitate the contact, but at the end of the day the children cannot be forced. If you stop contact your child's other parent may not do anything, but they could take you to court to reinstate access. Courts tend to want to encourage a relationship between the child and parent, but will listen to how the child feels, especially once they start to get older. This will usually involve a CAFCASS officer speaking to your child and observing each parent with the child.

6

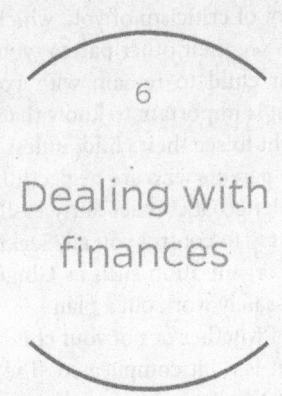

Dealing with finances

The financial implications of becoming a single parent are often a concern. Of course, this is going to depend on several factors including your own income, the available financial support and the number of children that you have. There may be significant differences depending on whether you were married, whether you have been bereaved, or whether you made the decision to be a single parent alone. Unfortunately, as discussed earlier, women who are single parents are one of the groups in society most likely to live in poverty. There are naturally exceptions to this, but due to many complexities in the possible financial support available for single parents, and challenges around balancing childcare and work, many find themselves living in precarious financial circumstances.

Why? Some of the reasons are obvious. If you are the sole adult in a household, there is either only one wage coming in, or you are trying to survive on financial support from sources like Universal Credit (or for many, a combination of both). Even if you only had one wage coming into the household

Dealing with finances

when you were in a relationship, often this means that childcare costs were reduced. Of course, theoretically, if your children are with you the majority of the time, you should receive financial support from the other parent. I'll come back to this later, but sadly many single parents find that this does not happen, or not in a reliable way. Even when it does, often it is simply not enough to meet the needs of a child. With the cost-of-living crisis in particular, many single parents even on higher-than-average wages are struggling.

Balancing work and childcare when you are the main parent can be incredibly tricky. One thing that always seems so unfair is that although non-resident parents are required in the UK (in theory at least) to financially support their children, there is no requirement for them to participate in any set amount of childcare unless court ordered. Financial support does reduce the more nights of care they give, but for those with more money there is little incentive to participate in childcare if they don't want to. Financial support is also reduced per night, meaning that if they wish to they could start their time with their children in the evening, missing the need to support after-school childcare and so on. Childcare costs are also not considered within financial maintenance.

Single parents are often told that they need to work to increase their incoming wage. However, when you have most of the responsibility for childcare that can be really difficult. Childcare can be hideously expensive and is often only offered during the day. Overnight care can sometimes be available but is often even more expensive or requires the support of a flexible (expensive) nanny at home. Once your children are in school you may be bound by whether there is an available spot at breakfast or after-school club. If school doesn't start until 8.45am and there is no breakfast club, how do you get to work for 9am? What do you do in the school summer holidays if you only have so much leave and there are no holiday play schemes available? And that's before we consider needing to have a day off because your child has picked up another bug (ironically at childcare).

On top of this, unfortunately childcare costs can be greater for those in lower-waged and more precarious jobs, which are typically less flexible. When I was first a single parent, I was an academic and I had the privilege of being able to be relatively flexible in the hours I spent at work. Yes, there was a huge amount of catching up on work late into the night, but I knew that many parents earning far less than me did not have that option. This meant that friends with lower-paying roles often had to spend more on childcare as they weren't able to have that same flexibility.

What financial support is there?

> *'Know your budget. It's better to understand where the financial pressure is rather than stick your head in the sand. Then seek support from the agencies that are out there to help – don't suffer in silence.'* Jess

The following sections are based on entitlements in the UK. It is likely that if you are based in another country there are similar sources to explore for the different elements considered below.

If you are the main caregiver for your children, you will remain eligible for their child benefit. However, one of the most rage-inducing changes to financial support for parents has been the reduction in child benefit when your earnings hit £50,000, tapering off entirely by the time you get to £60,000. Of course, if you are on a lower income this can seem like a *huge* salary, but if you are living in an expensive area and have high childcare costs, it can very quickly be swallowed

Dealing with finances

up. The main unfairness is that this limit does not take into account household income, but rather individual income. If a single parent earns over £50,000 their child benefit will start to reduce. However, if two parents together each have an income of under £50,000, so a joint income of £99,999, they will keep all child benefit.

Depending on your income and circumstances there are several avenues to explore for financial support. Even if you don't think you will qualify, it is worth looking at the Entitled To website www.entitledto.co.uk, which has a calculator that will identify everything you might be able to claim, taking into account circumstances like having a child with a disability. If you are on a low income you may be able to receive further support, including with housing and council tax. The Healthy Start scheme provides financial support which can be used to buy cows' milk, fruit and vegetables and first-stage infant formula. You can check your eligibility here: www.healthystart.nhs.uk. If you are ever struggling to buy food, speak to your health visitor, GP or Citizen's Advice. They may be able to refer you to a food bank. You can find more information on the Trussell Trust website www.trusselltrust.org/get-help. The Money Saving Expert website also has lots of ideas for reducing costs. Citizen's Advice can also help with benefits and savings.

> 'Don't be afraid to take what is on offer or think that by accepting it you are taking it from someone else "more in need than you". It's there and the system provides it so take it. You have contributed to a system all your life. Now it's time for it to help you when things are very hard.' Pete

If your partner has died, you may be able to access Bereavement Support Benefit (if they died prior to 6 April

2017 you may be entitled to Widowed Parent's Allowance). If you have children or you're pregnant, you can get a lump sum payment of £3,500 and monthly payments of £350 for up to 18 months. This payment is tax free but it clearly does not represent the support a partner would have provided if still alive. To qualify your partner must have either paid National Insurance contributions for at least 25 weeks in one tax year, or died because of an accident at work, or a disease caused by their work. Unfortunately, this is only if they were your partner when they died. You cannot access this if your child's other parent dies and you were divorced or not living together.

'I'm not entitled to anything because of my decision to go it alone. It's understandable as who would carry that cost, but also frustrating as I have no one else to rely on. Likewise, if I had become pregnant before my husband died, I would have received some support but only for a short time. I feel that it excludes some people from having these choices.' Rachel

Unfortunately, as Rachel describes there is no financial support system for single adoption or IVF by choice, other than more broadly if you are on a low income. This must limit who chooses these options and is able to proceed. It seems unfair that bereavement payments end so quickly too. Children don't stop having needs within 18 months of losing a parent and are likely still strongly feeling the impact of that loss.

'Don't limit yourself or panic. Don't think that just because you're single you will have to rely on universal credits forever, though it's also fine to if you're happy there. But believe in your own strength and capabilities.

Dealing with finances

Your career doesn't have to be over because you are a single parent if you don't want it to be'. Becky

Also, as Becky points out, remember that things are likely to change in the future. If you are reading this with young children or are just at the start of becoming a single parent, then you might be feeling absolutely overwhelmed and as if things will be difficult forever. Remember that children grow, childcare costs reduce, and children become more independent, which will likely give you more flexibility to increase your hours or change the type of work you do.

Support with childcare costs

The Entitled To calculator will estimate the support available for childcare costs. Even if you have a relatively high income you may be entitled to support with childcare through Universal Credit, despite not qualifying for more general support. Unfortunately, some people do fall into a tricky area where their earnings mean they are not entitled to support with childcare costs through Universal Credit, but they are also not earning a high enough income to feel that it is affordable. There is an option to explore the tax-free childcare scheme (available to all parents except those who earn over £100,000) in which you set up an online childcare account for your child. For every £8 you pay into this account, the government will pay in £2 to use to pay your provider (up to £2,000 a year, or £4,000 if your child has a disability). Both parents can pay into this account.

Arranging child maintenance

Child maintenance is a regular payment made to the parent who has more day-to-day responsibility for a child/children by their other parent. It is based on a calculation of how many nights the other parent has the child during a typical year and their income. It increases with each child. Your income has absolutely nothing to do with how much you are entitled to. There is a calculator available online at www.gov.uk/child-maintenance-service for you to work out your entitlement.

The figures calculated by the child maintenance service are meant to be based on the basic figures for supporting a child. Unfortunately, unless there is a court order in place, this amount is considered sufficient regardless of the *actual* costs of taking care of your child. For example, if you have two children and your child's other parent has an income of £35,000 and has them overnight every other week for two nights, then an estimated amount of maintenance would be £435. That works out at about £8 a day per child for the remaining 26 days of the month they are with you.

Of course, you can *request* that the other parent contributes to the full shared cost of their children. In an ideal world the true cost of caring for a child would be calculated and split fairly between parents, dependent on income and time spent looking after the child (which are often inversely related to each other). If you are able to approach them to suggest this, you might like to consider including elements such as childcare, clothing, bigger purchases such as bikes or laptops, school trips and, well, just the real day-to-day living costs of children, especially as they become older and attempt to eat you out of house and home. If considering additional payments it would be fair to take into account any financial support received through Universal Credit for childcare, but also to consider the impact on earnings of being the one mainly responsible for the children (as we discussed above).

The government prefers parents to come to an agreement about child maintenance between themselves. If you find

Dealing with finances

that you are not receiving child maintenance then you can contact the Child Maintenance Service (CMS), which will attempt to collect it directly from the other parent, through their payslips if in paid employment or through any benefit payments received. They also have the power to collect direct from bank or building society accounts or to take the parent to court. A charge can be placed on any property and they hold the ultimate power to disqualify the parent from driving or holding a passport, or even to send them to prison. However, in reality these options rarely seem to be used, with unpaid child maintenance adding up to around half a billion pounds in the UK.

Using the Collect and Pay service will incur a cost for both of you – something that feels deeply unfair if you are the one not receiving money that you are legally owed. At the time of writing this amounts to 4% of the maintenance amount for the parent receiving money and 20% for those paying it (or failing to). There is also a £20 application fee (although you are exempt if you have experienced domestic abuse or are under 19 years old).

Holes in the system

'Child is now an adult. Used to contribute the amount calculated by Child Maintenance but was regularly in arrears and tried to avoid paying when changing jobs. I don't feel it was a fair amount as it was very small and they did not have other children to care for and didn't buy anything extra the child needed either. However I feel proud that I supported the child anyway without much support.' Evangeline

Unfortunately, there are major holes in the child maintenance system, and it is a problem that disproportionately affects women. As above, the figure set by the Child Maintenance Service is the minimum cost that must be paid, with no legal obligation for the other parent to pay anything in addition. The system is deeply unfair in that there is no statutory requirement for the other parent to pay for childcare costs, although in some cases this has been ordered by a court (which is a drawn out, emotionally exhausting and expensive experience). Why it is not simply half the actual costs of caring for a child (taking into account childcare) I do not know.

> 'He contributes via the DWP because he's on benefits. It's a paltry sum of less than £7 a week. I lose some of it because I have to pay an administrative fee to even receive it, which I think is really unfair. He's never paid me enough to make a reasonable contribution towards our son's care. It's insulting and depressing, especially as I know the money comes from the taxpayer and not as a result of him having to say, release equity from his home or by selling stocks and shares that he profits from. I also know he has a business selling expensive goods on Facebook, but unless these things are declared to DWP/HMRC there's nothing I can do. He's fought me at every corner to not have to pay, or to pay as little as possible.'
> Martha

One of the biggest criticisms of the child maintenance calculations is that, depending on the other parent's earnings, they often do not cover half the cost of raising a child (assuming for now that half the cost is financial and not time). If their income drops or their circumstances change, then the amount they legally have to provide reduces. It also appears that there has been no 'cost-of-living crisis' increase. With inflation still in double digits in 2023 and huge increases in food prices, utilities and mortgage rates, the day-to-day costs of raising a child have increased, yet child maintenance rates have not.

There are also several factors which might reduce the child maintenance you receive, even though the costs of caring for your child do not decrease. If a parent goes to prison payments will stop. If they are not working and are receiving benefits you will receive a nominal amount per week, which is often around £7. Obviously a parent cannot give you what they do not earn, but there is no system for them paying you back once they are earning. They effectively have no financial responsibility for your child, while your responsibility continues. Going back to the previous idea of sharing the costs equally, I am unsure why a debt does not accrue instead.

Additionally, maintenance is based on the co-parent's salary only. If they move in with someone who earns more money it does not take this into account, despite a greater household income. If they give up their job and are supported by a new partner, even if this partner is a billionaire, there is no legal requirement for maintenance to be paid. At first glance this seems partly fair. After all, the new partner did not create your child. However, it appears that this 'fairness' only goes one way. If the parent who has more responsibility for the children receives any financial support, in terms of child benefit, tax credits or universal credit, this is reduced in line with any new partner's salary. Legally, however, there is no requirement for that new partner to contribute financially to the child at all. This creates a clear financial and power imbalance that predominantly affects women as they are most likely to be the ones with greater caring responsibilities for their child.

Maintenance also reduces if the other parent moves in with someone else who already has children, or has further children.

However, they are under no legal requirement to contribute towards those children. They may become financially better off by moving in with someone, yet they can then reduce how much they support their existing children financially. This can feel very unfair as of course it does not reduce the costs for your child. The equivalent would be the main caregiver being awarded more money if they move in with someone as they have more children to care for. Of course, this is seen for what it is – unfair. But why is it so accepted in the other direction?

Finally, if a non-resident parent becomes a full-time student supported by a student loan, that money is not counted as income for child maintenance purposes. Perhaps it is because it is a loan, but it seems unfair that a parent can opt out of financially supporting their child. But it gets worse. If the parent who has primary responsibility for the child chose to stop working and become a full-time student, they would be expected to support their child through their loan payments! If you make an application for Universal Credit as a full-time student '*Loans that cover maintenance, such as living expenses, rent and bills, will be deducted from your Universal Credit.*' So student loans are apparently the Schrödinger's cat of income. Both income and not.

How common are these tactics?

'He doesn't contribute financially. He did at one point via CMS. He then quit his job and flat out refuses to pay toward the girls. Has always protested against it and doesn't believe he should. Part of the reason he chose to have them so he would pay less to CMS.' Nicole

It is difficult to estimate how many families are affected by under- or non-payment of child maintenance. Data exists for parents who use the Child Maintenance Service to formalise

Dealing with finances

payments (either through Direct Pay or Collect and Pay), but this will skew the data as there are co-parents who organise payments between themselves, perhaps just using the online calculator as a guide. It is estimated that just one-third of single parents in the UK regularly receive the full amount of child maintenance due.[1] Similar rates are found in the USA,[2] although this rises to around half in Australia.[3]

One of the biggest issues is that when single parents do not receive support, the onus is often on them to chase it from the other parent or face this deduction. Many parents simply find this too frustrating, exhausting or time-consuming for the amount they think they will get. Many single parents also sadly find that their child's other parent will try to minimise income to avoid paying, or frequently change jobs or hours to cause chaos and a lag in payments. An Australian report exploring mothers' experiences of the child support system found that two-thirds felt that their child's father did this through cash-in-hand work, reducing income, early retirement, increasing pension contributions or putting assets in someone else's name.[4] Others found that the other parent simply lied by under-reporting income, or overstated the amount of time that they were caring for the children, which significantly reduced the amount of support owed.

Challenging this was a logistical nightmare to try to prove and simply wasn't worth it. One mother described how her ex-partner could just ring up and tell child support that he was seeing the children more often and the amount of support would be reduced. However, she couldn't simply counter the information in the same way and had to evidence that it wasn't true. Others were worried about repercussions if they challenged information. They worried that all support would be stopped, or that the parent would stop seeing the children in retaliation. Others didn't want to open 'old wounds' by getting involved in an argument. Parents who avoided paying child support often had a history of violence and aggression. They used avoidance of payment to continue harassing their ex-partner. Overall, pragmatically it felt easier to just go along with it, even though they knew that it was deeply unfair.

Some women in the survey didn't receive any financial support at all. When they tried to contact the Child Support Agency to report this, many found the process frustrating. Often significant time passed with no movement, and when they followed up they were made to feel as if they were the ones being unreasonable. Some were told that there was little the agency could do because the case was too difficult, or that they needed to return to court (at significant cost). One mother even reported being told that she should be grateful for what she did receive, while another was told not to rely on the money.

This issue, like many vulnerabilities in parenting, appears to have been made worse by the Covid-19 pandemic. In one UK study that interviewed 62 victim-survivors of economic abuse about their experiences of financial abuse during Covid-19, maintenance being stopped or reduced was a common theme. Among those female participants who were eligible for child maintenance payments, 84% were worried about receiving money owed. Of these women over a fifth reported that their payments had stopped during the pandemic, with a further 18% experiencing payments becoming unreliable. Typically, payments just stopped with no reason given and women were left to try to contact the Child Maintenance Service, often with little success. Most of the participants in this situation relied on the payments to care for their child day-to-day, leaving them unable to afford essentials as a result.[5]

You'll notice the use of the phrase 'economic abuse' in that study and yes, a co-parent refusing to pay child maintenance

Dealing with finances

that is due, using loopholes to reduce the requirement, or being deliberately unreliable in their payments, *is* economic abuse. Economic abuse is recognised in the 2021 Domestic Abuse Act as any behaviour that impacts on someone's 'ability to acquire, use or maintain money, property or obtain goods or services'.[6] This can include behaviours such as preventing someone from working, withholding information, damaging property, or taking out a loan in someone's name.[8] You do not need to be in a relationship with someone, or even ever see them for it to happen, and in many cases it actually starts *after* couples separate.

In one study in the USA with 22 women who were divorcing after experiencing abuse, 17 of them were experiencing some form of economic abuse from their ex-partner, such as hiding money or running up huge legal bills in an attempt to leave them with no money.[7]

Common effects included having to reduce how much was spent on children's activities, struggling to buy uniforms, reducing the food budget, getting into debt and borrowing from others.[8] Understandably feelings of anxiety, depression, guilt and frustration were very high among respondents, alongside a feeling of despondency and resignation. Mothers often described having to choose between the effort and emotion needed to fight any non-payments and the impact of not receiving the money. This fell hardest upon those who needed the money the most: being able to ignore it was seen as a privilege.

Steps you can take

'I used to ask him to contribute to things like their dance/ drama classes, football, and the epic annual new school uniform and supplies bill, but he used it as a method of control, so I no longer ask him for anything. It's not worth

> *communicating with him over. I will take care of my kids all by myself and when they grow into amazing humans, I'll take 100% of the credit.'* Becky

I wish I could write a simple section here with excellent advice on what you can do to ensure you receive the money you are owed. Unfortunately, as described above the system seems so rigged in favour of the paying parent that chasing payments from a parent who is determined not to cooperate is extremely difficult. Somewhat ironically, I added an HMRC link to a previous draft of this book on what steps you can take if maintenance isn't paid. It's been withdrawn and there doesn't appear to be an update. This feels illustrative of the whole issue.

Some potential suggestions:

- Remind your co-parent that they will pay more if money is collected via the CMS.
- You can try to collect evidence that they are likely being paid more. This is very difficult to prove, but you can challenge their accounts through the Child Maintenance Service by raising a complaint. Whether this will get a response or be actioned in any sensible time frame is another matter.
- Keep records of when you are caring for your children (and how much time the other parent spends with them). If they are being very difficult you might want to document this with photos in some way.
- If you are financially secure you might decide to cut your losses for the sake of your wellbeing. Of course, this isn't the right or fair response, but several of the parents contributing to this book decided that the very small amounts that they were receiving, the sheer stress

of trying to chase money down, or the control that it enabled simply wasn't worth it.
- Support the work of organisations fighting for fairness for single parents such as Single Parents Rights, found here www.singleparentrights.org. Write to your MP repeatedly about the unfairness of the maintenance system. There are actually now two All Party Parliamentary Groups relating to single parenting, including one aiming to tackle the non-payment of child maintenance. Find out more here: www.gingerbread.org.uk/our-work/policy-and-campaigns/all-party-parliamentary-groups-appgs

7
New relationships

Starting a new relationship after becoming a single parent can feel like a really daunting step. Of course, this will likely be heavily affected by the story behind how someone became a single parent. Bereavement can have its own set of challenges. Separating because of adultery or abuse has others. But even when a separation has been amicable, making the decision to move on and start a new relationship, however casual, with someone else can bring up a lot of emotions.

This book was never going to tell you what to do and how to feel when it comes to thinking about relationships. For a start, I'm not a relationship counsellor! But also, although there is some great advice out there about things to think about, I think deciding to move on (or not), how seriously, and how soon is very nuanced and differs according to your relationship.

The positives of new relationships

'I call him the upgrade as a joke, but in all honesty he really is.' Stacey

Dealing with finances

I'm trying to not make this section sound like '10 reasons you need a new man/woman', but I want to celebrate the positive ways new partners can add to our lives. There can be many challenges in blending families and often the stresses of this are highlighted, without also exploring the fact that many single parents go on to find new relationships and are happy, perhaps even happier than they were before. Of course, this can take time and trial and error, and it doesn't just magically happen without being open, honest and talking to each other. As with any relationship at any stage of our lives there are good, bad and ugly scenarios. It's about compatibility, timing and of course the luck of finding someone whose way of life, values and priorities also fit with yours.

1. The joy of a genuine partnership

    'He makes me feel safe and loved and I'd not experienced that before. It's taken some getting used to, being treated this way that is. It's different and sometimes it makes me quite emotional when I think about how different it is to past relationships.' Stacey

2. Connecting with another adult

    'I had forgotten how much I missed adult company. Knowing someone would be there in the evenings, having someone to mull over problems with, or simply being able to chat nonsense to. After a long day with children having someone there who would talk about something other than dinosaurs or Minecraft was a welcome relief!' Rebecca

3. Sharing the load

    'My current partner is the most equitable and hands-on man and father I've ever known. He treats my eldest

as his own and he is very involved in things like school, sports clubs, hobbies etc. He dislikes my son's father and now my partner is a father himself finds it frustrating and upsetting that our eldest could be so easily abandoned by his biological father. I am grateful that my partner is such a good father and role model to both of our boys.' Martha

4. Emotional support

   'I had a live-in partner when my daughter was younger and then got married to my now husband when she was 11. Both partners were/are very active in her life and did share the practical load of parenting. Husband totally shared the parenting – emotional, practical etc. I feel very lucky to have had a supportive partner.' Evangeline

5. Validating your experiences

   'I had a long-term relationship of about seven years although we did not live together. They were unimpressed with the absent nature of my son's father, as he was an active parent in his own children's life'. Jess

6. Helping to heal past experiences

   'I was very low after the experiences of my marriage and didn't have a high opinion of men. My husband gently showed me how things could be different. He treats me completely differently and has helped me to feel more confident in myself. I feel like a different person now with him and this has made me a better parent too.' Rebecca

7. Being someone reliable for your child

   'My daughters have struggled due to their mother's illness. She is sadly not able to be as reliable and loving as we would like. Sarah has changed all of that. I know

Dealing with finances

she finds it difficult at times, but she has been a constant for them and loves them deeply while also respecting the relationship they do have with their mother. I'm in awe and so grateful for how she has nurtured our girls.' <u>Chris</u>

Some of the challenges

'A single mum friend told me that I was brave for moving on with someone else – this seemed odd to me at first, but I see what they mean now – navigating parenting with someone who's not your child's biological parent is much harder than I expected it to be.' <u>Hayley</u>

I also want to highlight some of the challenges that parents experience when they decided to undertake a new relationship. Life isn't always easy and straightforward, and alongside the many joys of finding a new partner, there can be hurdles and challenges when adapting to your new normal, especially if you are blending families together. I think it's also important to explore these as it's validating to read if you feel that everyone around you is living the social media-style exciting and perfect relationship. If you're thinking about taking the next steps in a new relationship it can also help to be aware of some of the challenges that arise in new relationships when children are involved, because it can help to set your expectations of what is 'normal' without thinking that it is just you not doing it 'right'. This can also help you hopefully work through any difficulties, discussing them with your partner knowing that they are really common.

1. Losing your autonomy

    'It was no longer just me and the kids and that felt oppressive at times despite us having a great relationship. She felt the same.' <u>Dan</u>

One of the positives about becoming a single parent that many of the contributors to this book highlighted was the joy and feeling of control from being able to make decisions for your life with your child. Depending on the 'seriousness' of a new relationship, many parents found that changed. From spending more time together, to moving in, decisions need to be more flexible as a family unit and that can take some getting used to. Even when a new partner is not directly involved with parenting, tastes and preferences can obviously differ and small things you are used to doing together might need to change.

2. Balancing your children and partner

'I felt very protective about changing the kids' schedules or our little routines. I found it difficult to compromise because although I am quite laid back and don't tend to worry about the small stuff, it felt as if when I agreed to change things because he preferred to do it another way then I was being disloyal to my child. It felt like I was being pulled in two over pretty mundane stuff such as going out for breakfast or lunch.' Kirstie

Related to the challenge of losing full autonomy over your life is the uncomfortable experience of feeling torn in two over who to prioritise. To some extent this can exist in any relationship, but when you're in a relationship with the parent of your child it can feel easier to expect them to make some sacrifices in prioritising the needs of your child. When that person isn't their parent, and when it's also a newer relationship in which things might feel more fragile, or that you should be able to prioritise your partner, it can feel really difficult. You can feel like you're always letting someone down and that you're in charge of balancing everyone's happiness.

Dealing with finances

> 'My children struggled to share me with my partner at first. I needed to be careful to spend time with each of them one-to-one to ensure they felt loved and had my attention. It's a big change to juggle the maintenance of a relationship as well as caring for children, especially those who have had a difficult time.' Craig

This can be the case for time and emotional energy too. Perhaps you want to do all the 'new partner' things, such as going out for dinner or away for the weekend, but at the same time you feel guilty for not including your children. This can feel trickier if your partner doesn't have their own children or they've grown up. Theoretically they have the freedom to do what they want and it can feel like your responsibilities to your child are stopping you from having this experience. Maybe your child needs additional support due to neurodiversity, an illness or disability. Throw in the potential need to rely on an ex-partner to meet their responsibilities in caring for your child during your time away and it can feel a lot easier just to hide under the bed and never come out.

Of course, your new partner has chosen to have a relationship with you and your children as a package. Unless you hid your children until they moved in and acted surprised when they noticed they were there, they will understand that life will be a little more complicated than when everyone was younger and child-free. However, sometimes we don't realise the balancing that goes on with children until we live with them. So what's the main message? It is tricky. It takes compromise and a whole load of understanding on all sides. Talking usually helps. There's a big difference between hiding it all and saying 'No I can't do that,' and explaining more clearly by saying 'I would absolutely love to, but this is what I'm worried about'.

3. Different parenting styles

   'I lost the autonomy and, as there were other children in the family now, who had experienced very different parenting styles, there were compromises that had to be made and that was hard.' Evangeline

If you're bringing together children from two families, this can be a tricky as there are lots of different relationships to think about. Your partner's relationship with your children, your relationship with their children, and how all the different children get along. I've made this into a section itself further on in this chapter, but the challenge of differing parenting styles raises its head even with just one set of children.

4. Going too quickly or underestimating your worth

   'If I had my time again, I'd probably do things differently – I was advised by a bereavement therapist and my late husband's parents to start dating again before I was ready and I made some poor choices which probably didn't help either my daughter or myself.' Hayley

Go at your own pace. There is no need to jump in, make decisions that will last forever or get more serious than you want to. You've been through a lot. You can take your time, whatever others may think.

'I had a brief relationship which was full of challenges. A good friend sat me down and pointed out I was settling for less than I deserved. I think in a way I thought I had to compromise because of my story and history. I just was not ready really.' Rachel

Consciously or subconsciously, some parents might think that because they now come as a package with their children and cannot drop everything to meet the needs of a new partner, that they must compromise. Rubbish. A partner should make your life better. They should not make you feel like you are settling or should be grateful.

> 'I've been single ever since and have grown to love the relationship I have with myself. My mum is my main support, she helps with childcare and has been my rock in all ways possible. I'm eternally grateful. I absolutely couldn't fathom doing this with anyone else.' Nicole

Or indeed, remain positively single. Life doesn't need a romantic partner in it to be full.

5. Compromising on how involved a new partner will be

> 'Initially my new partner had a great relationship with my daughter and played an active role in her life but this has deteriorated over time. He doesn't contribute financially to my daughter's care, which is fair enough, she's not his child, but bereavement benefits stop when you move in with someone – this has never made sense to me, and penalises the child involved. Does the government really assume a new partner is going to financially subsidise someone else's child(ren)? Regarding the emotional load of parenting, I feel completely alone much of the time. Perhaps I was naive as I had wanted him to be a "proper" dad for her... things have improved recently but it's still not great.' Hayley

As always, there are no right or wrong answers here, but this can feel like one of the trickiest things about moving in together. Some of the trigger points can be around how much your new partner will care for your child, financially provide for your child and how much they will get involved with discipline. You might like to think about:

- *Caring for your child.* Are they comfortable caring for your child on their own or taking them out? Are you both equally free to go out alone, or is there an expectation that you must ask your partner to care for your child while they don't in return? How will this apply to things like the school run, haircuts or dentists' appointments?
- *Finances.* Who will pay for what? Does this differ when you're out for the day and have a meal together? How does a split in responsibility affect each of your finances?
- *Parenting role.* Will they be a parent figure, or more of a supportive adult, perhaps more reflective of an aunt/uncle role? They may feel more at ease with the second, or struggle with this because they feel that they're unable to react to your child. Equally you might feel discomfort if they discipline your child, or feel the burden if they get to be the fun person.

Only you and your partner can work out what feels right, and it is likely that it will change over time. Living with someone for a few months is going to be different to the relationship between your partner and children that will likely emerge after a few years. These conversations, although tricky, can help you work through your expectations and think about the experiences of the other partner. However, I stress that these responsibilities should feel fair and acceptable to you both. Although there may need to be some compromise, a partner should act like a partner. What I mean by that is that you should, within reason, be sharing and managing the

Dealing with finances

load together. Although it is all a continuum, it's going to start to feel very unbalanced if they take no role in childcare or sharing finances.

Ideally you will discuss these topics before your relationship becomes more serious. Your partner gets to lay out their preferences, you get to lay out yours and you can both make a decision going forward. Of course, it often doesn't work that way, as we don't tend to approach relationships like we do business opportunities. Your partner is not auditioning for employment. But please remember that a partner should make life better, and you deserve someone who genuinely shares your life (and all its nuances) with you.

Blending families together

If your new partner also has children, at some point you'll probably consider what your new family unit will look like going forward. Some couples choose to maintain separate homes, spending time in each other's homes with or without their children. Some might choose to move into one partner's home. Others might look for somewhere new together. Have I said that there's no right answer here, just the one that works best for you, enough times yet?

There are lots of things you might need to think about and here are some:

- *Age of children.* If your children are younger, you will likely be making more of a long-term decision about what your shared lives will look like. If some of the children are older and about to move out or go to university, then your housing decisions in the first instance may be different to how they might look later on when fewer permanent bedrooms are needed.
- *Sex of children.* Who can share a room? And for how

long? The NSPCC has some guidance, and housing legislation states that children of the opposite sex should not share a room when one is over age 10, while it is encouraged, if space allows it, for children over the age of 10 to have their own room regardless of sex www.nspcc.org.uk/keeping-children-safe/in-the-home/sharing-a-bedroom/#legal
- *How often everyone is together.* If you both have ex-partners involved in co-parenting, will you often have all the children in the house? Will you alternate weekends? Will there be set bedrooms? Who will get the bigger ones?
- *Who has what needs?* Do some children need more space and solitude? How do the kids get along together?
- *Where does everyone live?* How much upheaval might there be? Changing schools, hobbies or meeting new friends? If one family needs to move are they happy with that or do they see it as a compromise? Might you all move in somewhere else together?
- *History of any shared homes.* Moving into a house that someone has lived in for a long time and where they have made memories and routines is different to moving into a newer place. Moving into a home that someone shared with an ex-partner can bring up all sorts of emotions. But sometimes children need continuity.

Here are some ideas on making the transition to blended families easier from our parent contributors.

1. Learn as you go along

   'Our family dynamic is very good. We are parents to three children, and we don't hold notions being "step" this or

Dealing with finances

"step" that. We're just a family and love the three children equally and in different ways. There are times where we get the balance right and others not so but we learn. What is tricky are the sometimes invisible boundaries that we're not sure we should cross when parenting. With the older two should my opinion come first because they aren't Nic's biological children? I don't feel so, but we can get cautious sometimes in our approaches.' Pete

Blending a family together is unlikely to be smooth sailing all the way. There are going to be difficult points, with disagreements and tense feelings, and things you have to work out together. The main thing to remember is that all of this is normal and that even when you're moving in together without children, that can be difficult at times too.

2. Take your time

'I would say go slowly and realise that it's an ever-evolving process not a be all and end all from the start. Trust takes time, whether that's between you and your partner in parenting roles, between yourselves and each other's children and between the children.' Rebecca

This is such an important one, although what constitutes enough time will vary depending on your circumstances. If you've known someone for a long time before starting a relationship and already have a trust bond with them, you might move at a quicker pace compared to someone you'd not known before. You know your children's personalities and how they are feeling around your circumstances and change. Your own mental health and ability to trust might have been affected by past relationship experiences. There may be financial, location or job-related factors affecting this.

Basically, no one can say what speed you should move at but you. It doesn't have to be linear. You can make small changes and pause for a bit before moving on any further.

Accepted wisdom typically states that you should be secure in your relationship's future before introducing a new partner to your children, but that is going to depend on your children, their age, and how often they might see your partner. Will they be spending enough time with your partner to develop a bond? Not introducing a partner when you have a four-year-old tucked up in bed and a babysitter is a very different experience to having eagle-eyed teens who notice you don't usually wear that outfit when you go out with your friend.

Children can react differently to a new partner. Some might be completely indifferent, others welcoming and some not sure at all. Follow your child's lead, but also, if they are unsure or against it, explore why. It might be that they simply need more time. They might need some support in coming to terms with the idea of you having a new relationship and what that means (i.e. you are not getting back with their other parent).

Your child's reaction might be different if they are younger compared to a teen. Teens might react negatively, affected by the very idea of their parent having a sexual relationship. Younger children might feel that they are having to share you with someone new. However old they are, with a first new partner it's going to feel like new territory for everyone and it's normal for children of any age to feel a bit unsettled. Saying that, some children just really like having someone new around, especially if they're being extra nice to them to win them over. As Stacey joked about the first time her son met her partner:

'My son was really cautious of my new partner when they first met as you'd expect but turns out it only took an

extra-large ice cream with sprinkles AND a flake to make him see a potential advantage here.' Stacey

Some parts of blending a family might go at a quicker pace than others. Starting a new routine of brunch every Sunday morning, or a film and pizza night, is less daunting than stages such as your partner sleeping over every night, or changing bedrooms around. Bigger things such as potentially moving house or school will have more of an bigger impact. Thinking about how you might all feel about this, and openly recognising that you feel anxious or that you might each have worries, is an important step in moving forward together.

3. Recognise that things can change for children and how they feel about themselves

   'One thing we didn't initially think about was what bringing our children together might mean for how they saw themselves. My son was used to being the eldest but after Katy moved in, her son was. You might think this was a small thing but it felt big to him at the time, especially when it was brought up in arguments. We also had an issue when my daughter advanced above her son in karate and he felt he was no longer the one who was good at karate. It was a bit of a minefield at the time but we've all stumbled along, talking about things and reminding the kids that they are unique and talented in their own ways, but most of all an equal part of our family and loved.' Dan

When you blend a family together, it's important to stop and consider how this coming together might affect how children feel about themselves. As Dan describes above, is moving in together going to affect how your children might see themselves? Things you might like to think about are birth order (is someone new the eldest now? Or someone else the baby?), talents, clashes over timetables (who goes to watch the football practice in two separate places?) and even small things like what food you get for a takeaway. None of these are insurmountable, or even predictable, but being aware and talking to your child about them can help ease the situation.

4. Take the space you need, alone and together

'We both quickly learnt that we need time together and apart in different ways and that's okay. That can include time one-on-one with our biological children, time spent totally apart, time with each other's child alone and of course time just the two of us. This makes it sound as if we have a timetable but we've fallen into a gentle rhythm of having all these different combinations over the month and it works for us.' Craig

Relationships are important and spending time building them in different combinations pays off, although it can start to feel quite complicated if you overthink it! As Craig describes above, you don't need an actual daily schedule, but trying to make sure that you are able to spend some time in different combinations can really help in building those bonds and trust. It can feel important for children to feel that they still have 'access' to you on your own and that they don't have to share you all of the time. This doesn't need to be anything complicated or expensive; sometimes just watching a film or baking cakes together can go a long way. Don't forget about yourself in all this though – time spent alone, doing things you want to do, or simply without having to think about anyone else, goes a long way to protecting your wellbeing. This is a handy side-effect of focusing on your partner spending time alone with the children to build their bond.

5. Practicalities and emotions don't always match

'He moved into my house because it had more space but unfortunately our budget didn't spread to a house that would have offered equal space to all of our children. His children stayed overnight with us every other weekend, which was four nights a month. My children hardly ever spend a night away from here with their father. It made much more sense for my children to have the bigger rooms here and we were lucky enough to have space, with an attic conversion, so that his children could have a room each too, albeit ones that were much smaller. They were fine with this at first but once they were teens started to see the difference and it felt unfair to them. They did understand why but I guess also felt that their dad was already spending more time with other children and they got the bigger rooms.' Evangeline

Our feelings are not always rational and logical as adults, let alone when some teenage hormones are thrown in. Talk to your children about your reasoning and say that if finances were different you would want more options to be available. Recognise and validate how they feel while also calmly sticking to the reasons for your decisions.

6. Recognise your children also have other relationships

'We made an effort to be positive and laid back about anything our children shared about their other parent, step-parent and step-siblings. It was complicated enough for us blending families but our children ended up being part of two blended families, going from having just one

sibling each to living with three or four new children in different combinations in the space of a few years. We were lucky that everyone got on okay but we also helped that by making the decision to always be positive and never criticise or interfere. We wanted the children to feel like they could talk to us about anything and that we respected that they had all these other relationships away from us too. It wasn't easy and at times I felt jealous myself when my children talked about their stepmother or siblings but in a way it also helped me realise better how my children probably felt in relation to my relationship and his children'. Rebecca

An added layer to think about is how your newly blended family might affect your children's other relationships with their other parent… and their other parent's potential new relationship. As Rebecca describes above, if you are feeling overwhelmed by the combination of relationships between yourself, your children, your new partner and their children… your children quite possibly have further layers of new relationships too, with their other parent's new partner and potential children. Even if things are going well they may worry about how you feel about these new people and feel reluctant to share as they might not know how you will react. Usually it's recommended that you try to remain calm, interested and supportive of anything your child tells you about their home life, which will help your child to feel more relaxed and keep talking to you.

It's completely normal to have moments of feeling jealous of the bonds your child creates in another family. It can help to try to remember that your child having a good time, feeling relaxed and trusting someone else is all positive. This is what you want, even though it can sting. Sometimes, your child

Dealing with finances

doesn't settle in a new household and is reluctant or refuses to go there due to relationships at that home. This can be tricky. If you can talk to your ex-partner amicably about this, do so and see if you can come up with some solutions to help them feel more settled.

PART III
SUPPORTING YOU AS A SINGLE PARENT

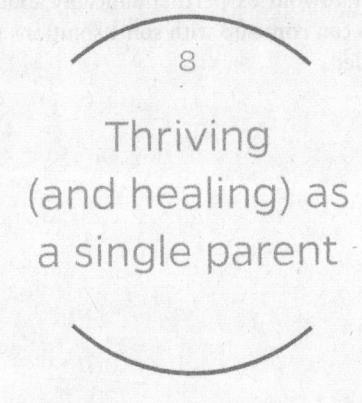

8

Thriving (and healing) as a single parent

So much of what is written about the topic of single parenting focuses on supporting children through separations or bereavement. But although important, they are only one part of the story. You deserve to be supported too, and to have your needs met in your own right, not just because your children benefit from you feeling the best you can. The whole experience of single parenting, even under the most amicable circumstances, can throw up so many feelings. You have the stress of adapting to your new life, the increased feelings of responsibility and any challenging emotions that have gone alongside the split. It can also trigger feelings that are more buried, from our childhoods or past experiences, especially around loss, abandonment and unfairness. All in all, taking care of your mental health, as much as you can, is important.

A common analogy is the idea of a flight attendant reminding you to put your own oxygen mask on first before you help others, or in other words, how can you look after your children if you don't care for yourself first? Although this is true, and can sometimes be a useful way of thinking, others feel that it diminishes the importance of your wellbeing as a person. So much of single parenting is about sacrificing things you want to do, or plans that you have, and instead pouring energy and time into your children. When we tell people that it's important they look after themselves for the sake of their children, this can feel like a whole new level of pressure and blame, especially if they're struggling.

So this chapter is going to explore some of the things you can do, because you matter. End of sentence. I realise that not everyone will be able to try all the ideas due to time, finances and other responsibilities (or will want to), but hopefully most will find something that resonates.

Take one day at a time

'Just take one day at a time, you will get through this – as long as you are both fed and safe at the end of the day, you've done great.' Hayley

If you're right at the start of your single parenting journey, or indeed further along and riding waves of grief or anger that come and go, be gentle with yourself. Try not to worry about the future or problems that haven't arisen yet. Breathe.

'I would like to reassure anyone that while it feels like you're in an unimaginably dark and difficult place, there is always light after dark. Take each day as it comes and don't get caught up in catastrophising, you cannot control everything! Some days are just about survival, and doing the bare minimum is fine if it gets you all safely through the day.' Martha

Your children will not be little forever. Your ex-partner will not always have control over you. You will heal and change. You will meet new people and experience new things. Life moves on and there is so much left to experience.

Know that 'good enough' parenting is brilliant

I raised this in Chapter 1, but it's important to remember that you don't have to be a perfect parent to be a good parent. You don't have to be better than other parents to make up for a feeling of loss for your child. You in yourself are enough. I always refer to the work of Donald Winnicott at this point. Winnicott was a paediatrician who coined the phrase 'good enough mothering' back in the 1950s. It was based on his observations of mothers and babies and his conclusions that mothers didn't need to perfectly meet the needs of their babies all the time in order for their babies to be happy and secure. In fact, some 'disappointments', as he called them, i.e. not reacting immediately, or getting it wrong, helped babies adapt to life. This belief in 'good enough mothering' has expanded in the last few decades to include parenting more broadly.[1]

If you're still struggling, could you ask a trusted friend to list the positive qualities they see in you? If you don't feel comfortable doing this, try to step outside yourself a little and imagine you are talking to yourself as a kind friend. What do they see in you? We keep repeating this but treat yourself with the kindness with which you would treat a good friend. Would you judge them if they messed up or weren't 100% on the ball all the time? No? So don't do it to yourself.

Don't compare yourself negatively to other families

'I used to buy into the comments and worry that our lives were more chaotic or unhappier than others, but

whatever is going on I realised that our home is much calmer just the two of us than it was when things were difficult. A good friend also helped me see that two-parent families experience lots of challenges too and that some families would be jealous of how calm our house is. Not every problem we face is because I'm a lone parent'.
Lauren

Time for a cliché, but it's the truth – comparison really is the thief of joy. Your life may well be very different to two-parent families, but that doesn't make it worse.

Work out who your people are

'I very quickly worked out who was really going to be there for me and who wasn't. Sadly some people seemed to disappear away and others offered help but you know didn't really mean it. But I had a few friends who I knew I could ring in an emergency because I needed something at 8pm or really needed help to look after them the next morning. These friends were small in number but the ones who really counted.' Stacey

In a world of social media, we have more 'friends' than ever, but how many of them are truly there for us? How many would drop everything if we had a true emergency, or go out of their way to help us when we're in a fix? Usually you can count these people on one hand. They are the ones that know us well, care for us and will be there to reassure us when we've had a terrible day. Yes, they might be gently honest with us, but we know they will always be on our side, willing us to do well. These are the people who matter.

> *'One of the things I found difficult was needing reassurance when your child is angry with you or upset but having no one at home to talk to. Talk through your parenting decisions with people you trust – although there are definitely good things about having autonomy, we should all check our own opinions and decisions at times. Keep talking to supportive friends and family. Even if it's just a short conversation. Adult relationships are important.'* <u>Jennie</u>

Talk, talk, talk and then talk some more to those trusted people. Ask their opinions, bounce ideas off them, share in the triumphs and lows of the day. You need friendships as much as your children do – don't be scared to spend time talking and offloading to others.

...and who your people aren't

> *'I found a lot of people pitied me or appeared to. Some revered me as a superhero. Others thought I was crazy and alienating the other parent.'* <u>Martha</u>

The world is full of people who want to criticise us and bring us down and sometimes it feels like single parents are an easy target. Perhaps you read a ridiculous headline in a tabloid that blames single mothers for everything wrong in the world. Perhaps you have an argument with your ex-partner, and they call you a terrible parent. Perhaps your child is behaving in a very difficult way and you blame yourself and the separation. Who do you know is going to be on your side?

In her book *Daring Greatly* Professor Brené Brown[2] talks about how she carries a small piece of paper in her wallet listing the names of the people whose opinion actually matters to her. If you're not on that list you're not getting into

Brené's head. Who would be on your list? Family? Friends? Your children? You get to choose, but don't let anyone who doesn't have your back on to the list. Similarly, in her book *The Light We Carry* Michelle Obama talks about the people who sit around her kitchen table.[3] She means this literally, but also uses the kitchen table as a metaphor for those who come into your home and head and support you unconditionally.

Remember that your emotions matter too

'Try to not suppress your feelings. Some days are just rubbish and give yourself permission to feel that. You don't have to put a brave face on and it takes energy you need. Wear your feelings. If you find yourself laughing enjoy it. You're entitled to as a bereaved person. Their death didn't not remove your entitlement to have a sense of humour. Funny things are still funny. Allow yourself these things.' Pete

It's so easy to forget about yourself, especially at the start and during your transition into single parenting. So many people ask you how the children are, or worse imply that they *will* be struggling, without consideration for how you are. But you matter. Feeling those emotions, taking time to process them, and taking time for yourself to do things that help you feel better, are all important. It doesn't have to be about your children all the time.

Do what you can to calm your system

'It's easier to spend time on me now the kids are teens but I always tried to prioritise at least a small amount of time for me when they were younger. I was lucky enough to be able to juggle my hours at work so I had a small

window about twice a week where I went swimming, to the gym or to walk in the woods. Anything that was about moving my body. I could have picked up the kids earlier from wraparound care, but I scheduled this as a non-negotiable as I felt much calmer afterwards. Not every second of spare time has to be about them.' Kirstie

I'm not going to suggest expensive massages and spa days here as the go-to answer for stressed parents. If you have the money and time (and like them), that's brilliant. But finding the time, money and headspace for these things can feel impossible when you're in the thick of it with small children. And sometimes being touched is the last thing you want! But if you can find the time to do something that helps to calm your system, this can go a long way to helping you feel generally less on edge. As Kirstie says above, always remember that putting yourself first is okay, and it is important, especially when you have no one else to pick up the load.

'Take a deep breath, go outside from time to time and scream, do something for you however tiny... read a page of a book, phone a friend, eat a piece of chocolate, have a latte, literally go and smell the roses, exercise, watch your child sleeping...' Elizabeth

Exercise is one idea. It can help increase energy levels over time, reduce stress and protect your health. It doesn't have to be intense – anything that raises your heart rate helps, whether that's joining a class, hiking in the woods or strength work. I know getting regular exercise can feel overwhelming as a single parent, especially with young children when you're doubly exhausted and it's difficult to leave the house. One silver lining of the pandemic was an increase in online classes that you can do anywhere. There is also a growing collection of accessible classes that are more inclusive and adapted to different disabilities, including seated yoga and tai chi.

Another suggestion is trying to prioritise time outdoors (green space) for you all. Research shows how much it can help reduce stress, free up headspace and help to reduce symptoms of anxiety and depression.[4] It doesn't have to be 'exercise' to get these benefits. Apparently cold-water swimming (known as blue space) has all sorts of health benefits including increasing dopamine, serotonin and endorphins, and reducing stress hormones, but I personally remain unconvinced![5]

If you feel very stressed, anxious or like panic is setting in, there are things you can try at home that can help relax your system. Self-massage can help reduce blood pressure, lower stress hormones and reduce symptoms of depression.[6] Meditation can help to make you feel calmer and more grounded, although I know how much of a struggle this can be when you have approximately 400 thoughts racing through your mind.[7] You could also try mindfulness techniques to counteract this and there are lots of free resources online.[8]

Grounding techniques can help too. Sit quietly and notice the things around you. Pick either a colour or a sense (i.e. sound) and name what is going on in your environment. You might choose five things that you can see that are green. Five things you can smell. Five sounds you can hear. This helps calm your system and bring you back to the moment. Another thing that can help is a yoga breathing exercise called alternate nostril breathing. To do this you use your thumb to close one nostril and breathe slowly and steadily out of the other one. Then switch. And repeat a few times. Keeping your eyes closed can help. The exercise focuses on steadying your breathing and calming your system.

Write, paint, be creative

> *'Write!!! If your head is full of feelings and you can or can't make sense of them write it down, type it, put a note on your phone and just let it flow. It's a great release valve and very undervalued in this situation.'* Pete

Some ideas might include a reflective journal or a diary for your children (you could choose to give this to them in the future, or not), painting, knitting and crochet, poetry and writing. Being creative is not only enjoyable but also has lots of proven health benefits.[9] It can help to distract you from unwanted thoughts, give you a feeling of accomplishment, and keep you busy in the evenings if your children are small and the evenings feel long. If you're stuck for ideas there is lots of inspiration to be found in *Maternal Journal* by Laura Godfrey-Isaacs and Samantha McGowan. Although aimed primarily at pregnant women and new parents, there are lots of ideas regardless of your age or gender. I'd recommend it to anyone wanting to increase their creativity.

Be aware of the signs that you might need some more support

> *'Seek therapy or counselling and attend regularly, so you have a safe and neutral space to work through your feelings. Let yourself feel whatever you feel – it's a grieving process. You grieve the loss of your relationship but also the loss of the future life you were going to have. You're not alone.'* Martha

Sometimes life just has its ups and downs. Single parenting can have lots of understandable frustrations. Sometimes talking to good friends is enough, but sometimes you might need some additional support and therapy can help. If you feel this would

Thriving (and healing) as a single parent

help you do not listen to any voices in your head that say you should be focusing your time, energy or potentially money elsewhere. Again, you matter. Your mental health matters and there are lots of different people who can help you with that. Some of the resources at the back of the book offer free support and recommendations for different services.

Sometimes, though, things can become more serious. Bereavement, past abuse and infidelity can have devastating consequences for your wellbeing. If you are still having to deal with an abusive or simply difficult co-parent, this can feel like it is wearing you down day after day, with your body never getting a chance to come down from that anxiety. Being able to spot the signs of anxiety, depression and trauma and reaching out for help from your GP is very important. Some of the common signs of anxiety and depression are:

- Feeling tense, nervous or tearful
- Feeling angry or frustrated
- Low confidence and self-esteem
- Being unable to relax and fearing the worst happening
- Worrying about the past or future
- Not being able to sleep or eat (or eating or sleeping more)
- Having difficulty concentrating
- Feeling on edge or lacking energy
- Intrusive traumatic memories or obsessive thoughts
- Not getting any enjoyment out of life or feeling hopeless
- Having suicidal thoughts or thoughts about harming yourself

If you have experienced, are still experiencing, or are wondering while reading this book whether you have experienced physical, sexual, financial or emotional abuse from a former partner, you may also wish to consider the Freedom Programme. It can help you work through your experiences, see behaviours differently and understand what has happened: freedomprogramme.co.uk. The NHS also has a list of resources for seeking further support with abuse: www.nhs.uk/live-well/getting-help-for-domestic-violence.

> Don't listen to that inner critic
> Dr Marianne Trent, clinical psychologist and author of *The Grief Collective*.
>
> It's fair to say that as humans we all have the potential to be our own harshest critic. As parents we have a whole host of things to grapple with and care about. Every now and then we might get a screaming reminder that it's no longer our sole responsibility to try and wear a top without a toothpaste stain on the front, eat a bit of fruit every now and then and look both ways when crossing the road: now, apparently, we have the responsibility for the nourishment and safekeeping of entirely separate people with at times very wilful minds of their own! It's not easy at all and of course our ability to grapple with all of this stuff is going to vary from day to day, heck, even minute-to-minute sometimes. Our abilities will depend on how well resourced and rested we are and what additional stressors we've got going on. And of course, the reasons why someone is a single parent to begin with can vary so wildly from person to person and might include: personal choice, infidelity, trauma, bereavement, domestic violence and more. The very reason, or reasons, why you're a single parent to begin with could well

contribute to how able to cope you feel. It might also mean that you've got some external criticism or echoes of previously traumatic criticism to contend with too. You may also feel that you're not measuring up well against 'the other parent' or even fantasy or imagined 'other parents' by not having as much money, time or support. A single parent is not always a lone parent but, in some cases, you might be juggling all of the balls with zero support from friends or family. Speaking to you as a mum and not just a psychologist, that is really the toughest load to carry. All of these factors can serve to amplify guilt and shame. So, that's a cheery read, isn't it? What can I suggest which might give you some practical pointers to shrink those complicated feelings down to size?

The first is that it is important to try to be on your own team. We have these fantastically complicated brains which have the ability to be violently self-critical. One of the most helpful things I have ever done for myself as a parent and a human is to welcome self-compassion into my life and continue to use it. Cutting yourself some slack, validating, giving yourself the advice you'd give to a best friend and attempting to self-soothe rather than further activate your already overloaded threat system with self-criticism or even at times self-loathing can be a transformational daily practice. To learn more about compassion I'd recommend listening to *The Compassionate Mind* by Paul Gilbert.

Take comparison off the table. We have the ability to compare ourselves to others and wow can we be good at it! When it comes to measuring up against co-parents, step-parents, or even what's-her-face from down the road, it's rare that we are feeling smug by the end of it. We are more likely to focus on the things we see as aspirational or must-haves and we often forget to draw upon our own strengths, which might be highly revered by others but may not be the type of thing you'd usually think to feature on your CV! These might include giving the best cuddles, helping your child feel calmest and safest and building the best cushion forts!

In a similar vein we can get really preoccupied with the idea that our own and our children's lives would be better if… However, my experience with working with a whole range of people across the lifespan have demonstrated to me that good enough is enough and anything else is a frilly bonus. Good enough includes consistency, predictability, and routine. In theory this might look like: regular bed, waking and meal times, knowing who will pick them up from school that day, knowing there will be food available at meal times, having the knowledge that it's safe to sleep and that when a child or young person wakes or returns from school their whole life won't be different by way of people moving in or out of the home and that they don't need to stay awake in order to safeguard a parent. It's likely that you already do most if not all of these things, and likely haven't ever once thought of them as a 'good thing'. It's time to start drawing upon these seemingly basic principles as real strengths, which will really help you and your children to thrive right now and in the longer term too.

I'd not be doing my job if I didn't mention that if your thoughts start to feel darker or bleaker, or if you begin to have thoughts that others would be better off without you, please contact your GP or local mental health team for the support and care which you deserve.

Lastly, I can't stress enough the importance of finding your tribe. Having a person or people you can talk to without judgement is so important. I love watching *Motherland* and how the friendships deepen, and the relationships become more honest as the episodes progress. While we may not all have hours to spend in the local coffee shop we can use WhatsApp, Messenger, and actual chats with people to help us to feel more connected with others. Similarly, if you do have good and trusted people in your life, please know it is okay to ask them to do things for you and then see point one about not feeling guilty about it either.

9

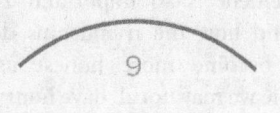

Practical tips for managing single-parent life

Parenting is hard however you look at it. Parenting without another adult in the house can feel like a whole other level of hard. There are the obvious big things of juggling finances and working out when on earth you are going to get a break. But there are the smaller things too. I think most parents have had the experience of a child announcing at 9pm that they have cookery class the next day, but it's a lot easier to pop out to the shops if you have someone else in the house.

However, as always, it's a bit more complicated than late-night trips to the supermarket, isn't it? On the surface, single parenting is about taking care of your child or children on your own. Or later on, maybe adapting to having a relationship and perhaps further still blending your lives together. Those are just the day-to-day practicalities though. Single parenting is about more than the experience of caring for children alone. It's how you feel, the difficult experiences that you carry with you and the worries that you have. Sometimes I think dealing with those is far harder than working out how you're going to get the remaining ingredients for your child to make a stew tomorrow.

There's a lot written about helping your child to adapt to separation or the loss of a parent. But what about you? What can help? I asked the parent contributors to this book about their top tips for juggling life looking after children alone, but also about how they look after themselves.

1. Stock up your cupboards

'I became a hoarder of food when I became a single parent! I could no longer just pop to the shops when I wanted, particularly after bedtime! So, money allowing, I made sure I always had a good supply of food, medication and general snacks to avoid that problem!' Jess

This is less of an issue these days with online deliveries that can often get supplies to you the same day if you live in a city. Card payments and online bookings take the pressure off. But paying for things to arrive speedily often has an increased cost and sometimes isn't possible. Knowing that you have a back-up in the house that you can use without having to even think about bundling the kids up and going back out can be very reassuring.

I realise that this adds a further financial load, and you may be struggling to afford what you need immediately, let alone any 'just in case' items. It could be something you work towards, or if any well-meaning person asks what they can do to help you could ask them to get you something that you need. Make an Amazon wish list or a simple long-life food shopping list for a supermarket that delivers and point people in that direction.

A list of things you might find it useful to work towards:

Why Single Parents Matter

- Cupboard foods so you can make a few meals if unable to get out to the shops. Include some things that you like and that might help you feel better after a bad day. This can also feel reassuring if you worry about money as you know you always have some food in.
- Spare toiletries such as toilet roll, nappies, sanitary protection, and toothpaste. Basic medications and supplies such as painkillers, antihistamines, antibacterial cream and plasters. You might want to include less common but urgent things like headlice treatment and cystitis sachets. Anything that can't wait a bit if you run out at 9pm when the kids are in bed.
- A stockpile emergency child cupboard. A glue stick, AA batteries and paper/printer ink. Some basic birthday cards and presents for parties that your child tells you about the day before. Random dressing-up clothes you can wear for any 'day'. Face paints solve a lot of problems.
- A small emergency fund that you don't touch – enough for a taxi if your bank balance is dry or some coins if your child declares at 8am that they need £1 for the cake sale.
- Perhaps this is a more expensive idea, but if your child grows predictably, it can be useful and reassuring to have a school uniform set waiting in the next size up, particularly for trousers/skirts that suddenly don't fit. Keeping old shoes as spare can also be an emergency solution when they suddenly lose one (more common than you think!).

2. Accept the help people offer

    'If friends or family offer support don't be ashamed to accept it, and be specific ("I really need someone to defrost my freezer"). Martha

Practical tips for managing single-parent life

How many of us struggle with this one? So often our natural reaction to being offered help is to say 'Oh no, I'm fine' despite everything collapsing around us. But one of the most helpful things you can do is to fight that urge and take people up on their offers. It might take some practice with those you trust, but most people who offer help do want to do something. Let them.

> *'I'd say to ask for help when needed, I definitely could have asked for more help over the years. The worst someone can say is no.'* Nicole

And if we're really being brave here, ask for help from friends and family before they even offer. Just because they don't offer to help, doesn't mean that they don't want to. Often we don't see the challenges that other people are experiencing and I think this can be especially true for people who don't have experience of single parenting.

Sound tough? That's because it can feel that way, at least at first. Many of us have difficulty accepting the help people offer, but this can be exacerbated by the experience of becoming and being a single parent. There can be a tendency to try to toughen up and be independent because you feel like you are the only person you can trust. You may have heard of the term 'co-dependency', when people are so closely entwined with someone else that they struggle to function without them. What is less well-known is the term 'counter-dependency', which is the opposite. It makes you feel scared by the idea of relying on others, as you might struggle to trust them and don't like asking for help. It can develop as a consequence of being let down by a partner, either during a relationship or afterwards, and can be high among single parents.

If you are worried about being a burden on others, or feel

that you should be coping, stop! It's not just okay to need support right now – you *deserve* support right now. Support is an important part of looking after yourself and making sure you are healthy and well enough to care for your children. I wouldn't say it's non-negotiable, as of course you can technically cope without support, but it makes things easier. A lot easier.

3. Find other people who understand

'I don't feel anyone truly understands what it is like to adopt unless you have adopted. For me a big struggle was going to parent and toddler groups – this was something I was so excited to do as I would finally be seen as a mum – but I discovered all a lot of "mums" do is talk about breastfeeding, moan about partners, relive pregnancy and birthing positive and horror stories and when they are having the next one – there wasn't one subject matter that I felt I could join in and I ended up just being with my daughter at the sessions and not making any "mum" friends.' Karyn

Sure, you have your friends who don't have children and your friends in partnerships who support you and your children. But with the best will in the world, they might not fully understand how you're feeling and what you're going through. Look for those connections – other single parents, bereaved parents, adoptive or solo parents. Of course, you won't gel with everyone just because of those things, but it can really help when you need someone who just gets it.

4. Build a childcare circle

'Definitely think about extending your childcare circle. Write a list of all your friends you can ask to have your kids when you need them to, seek out teenage babysitters

Practical tips for managing single-parent life

in your local area. Find as many people you can call upon if you need to as you can.' Becky

You need time for yourself. Whether that's time for a hobby, to date, or simply to sit in silence, your mental health and wellbeing matter too. Do not think twice about taking the opportunity to spend time doing what you need to do for yourself. If you are lucky enough to have willing family living close by, take them up on offers to help. Maybe you might pay for some extra time for your child at childcare. Are there any responsible babysitters in your area really wanting to earn a bit of money? If your budget doesn't allow, is there any option to work flexibly so that you can have a regular afternoon off? Setting up a childcare circle with friends where you look after your children and their children at the same time can work well (especially in the evening, when you can at least hope they will all sleep).

The main thing is to never feel guilty for doing this. Most parents want a break and time for themselves, but the difference when you are parenting alone is that you are the only person responsible for everything, including all the questions and mental load. You don't get an opportunity for micro-breaks, like when one parent does bath time or takes the children out on an errand. See it as an investment in everyone if you can't quite bring yourself to prioritise yourself just yet.

5. Sort out legalities

'I was hospitalised when my youngest was five weeks old, I had a perforated bowel and nearly died. This was a pivotal point for me to maximise my health and wealth and make sure my children had what they needed if I was no longer around. I also made sure I had a will in place and the necessary legal framework required.' Nicole

No one really wants to think about this, but once it is in place it can feel reassuring. If the worst happens, who would you prefer to care for your children? Do you have any particular wishes? How will that be funded? Not everyone is able to get affordable life insurance cover, but it is worth exploring if you can. Make a will, even if you don't think you have anything of financial value to leave to your children. If you do, whether that is through life insurance, work death benefits (worth checking out in detail) or property/savings, how would you like that to be split, when would your children be able to access it and who will be their guardian in the meantime? If you're struggling for money, some charities and businesses run a free will-writing month each year.

6. Connect with organisations

'Online single-parent/widowed parent communities like WAY (Widowed and Young) were so important in navigating the early years of bereavement and being a single mum. My city has a single-parent network which organises meet-ups for single-parents and their children – this was brilliant when I moved there and didn't know anyone.' Hayley

'Reach out to other single parents/adopters – online forums are amazing and just reading about others' perspectives and experience makes sitting on the sofa at night less isolating. The groups I am part of and accounts I follow are open and honest and raw and this has helped me not to feel isolated and overwhelmed as there is someone who is feeling similar to me. Go to your local adoption agency get-togethers and embrace the adoption world for you and your child, there is nothing more comforting for a child than to go to a Christmas party

with 100s of adoptive families for a little one to not feel different or alone.' Karyn

Depending on your circumstances, your people may be really specific. This might be related to your parenting role i.e. finding other single-parent friends who just understand, or other parents who have been bereaved. It might be to do with other elements of your life, such as a challenge your child experiences, or a health issue you have. The main message is about finding those people who understand you and what you're experiencing.

7. Remember to have fun with your child

    'Socialise with your child! Spend quality time with your child – it's hard when you're with them all the time and you have to do all the practical things to remember this, but it's really important. You need to have fun with your child! It doesn't matter if your house is a bit untidy – as long as it's clean enough and your child is safe there are other priorities!' Jennie

This is especially true if you are the one doing the majority of the day-to-day care and playing at bad cop/boring parent while a co-parent is off being the exciting Disney one. Other stuff can wait.

8. Make time for yourself – that's about you

    'When it comes to evening habits, for example watching you favourite programmes can create a lot of loneliness because they aren't there to share the likes, dislikes and chatter anymore. Stick on something or box sets that they had no interest in or really didn't like. Then it's about your

> *time rather than lost time with them. I binged* Game of Thrones *and* Boardwalk Empire *for example.'* Pete

Pete talks about forming new routines and habits after his wife died that didn't trigger painful memories. If you've separated from a partner the same applies. What can you watch or do that's just for you and isn't about being mum/dad?

Saying all of that...
> *'Just wing it. You'll be fine. Just keep showing up for your kids every single day and love them unconditionally. That's all you can do. The rest is just about rolling with the punches.'* Becky

10

How to support a single parent

This chapter goes out to all those who know and love single parents. Hopefully if you've read the rest of the book you'll have a good idea of the challenges that single parents can face. If you're wondering how you can help, here's a list of suggestions from my parent contributors about the supportive things that other people have done for them. If you're reading this as a single parent, here's your handy chapter for when people ask 'What can I do to help?'

1. Give unconditional emotional support

   'I have a small circle of very close friends who support me, listen to me, check in on me and love me unconditionally.'
   Becky

2. Don't disappear

   'There were some friends who just disappeared while others stepped right up. It wasn't who you thought it would be either, I was quite shocked.' **Lauren**

Why Single Parents Matter

3. Know that the little things matter

   'The kindest thing anyone ever did was to give me a little 'mother's day' teddy when my daughter was two years old and I'd never had a mother's day present. I found that incredibly touching.' Elizabeth

4. Give them the gift of time to themselves (but also know when to open your arms)

   'My sister and Mair's sister gave and helped so much in the early years which allowed me to get breaks and carve out time for myself to be social, to have me time, to go away for a few days. However, people knew when to include us. My friends knew I faced going back to an empty house so they were keen to often have us around for tea to lessen the void.' Pete

5. Don't exclude them just because they don't have a partner

   'Don't not include me because I don't have a partner. We're not at a 1950s dinner party! I'm still me and can talk to people in relationships.' Rachel

6. ... and make plans that they can join in with

   'Invite me to socialise WITH my child. Give me an opportunity to talk things through. Just coming round to care for the baby while I slept. Make me food!' Jennie

7. Don't just ask 'how can I help' – go do something useful

   'One of the best things a friend did when I moved into my new house was to go and do a shop for me to make sure I had all the basics in. She didn't ask, she just showed up.

How to support a single parent

It might just have been some tins of soup and pasta and things to her but to me it was a lifesaver when I got home and realised we needed something for dinner.' Rebecca

8. And particularly get stuck in at crisis points

   'When I moved into my new home all my friends rallied round to help with practical help with childcare and donations of furniture and unpacking, to emotional support by coming over to drink wine and eat cake. I felt like I was lifted up by my group of strong female friends and that support has carried me throughout the last decade.' Jess

9. Don't expect them to support your emotions

   'My mother was distraught at my divorce. I think she carried a lot of stigma from her earlier years and seemed hung up on what everyone would think. I however was not the person to complain to. Always complain outwards i.e. to those less impacted by the situation than you!' Kirstie

10. ... or side with the other parent

    'My own mother directly and indirectly hinted that this was all my fault, and I should have been a better partner. She then proceeded to be really nice to him, claiming it was about keeping our family unit together, despite him leaving. It broke my heart.' Evangeline

11. Support their decisions

    'Please simply support how I parent and know I'm making the best choices for me and the girls.' Craig

12. ...and most of all just be there

'The friends who sat with me while I worked through the stacks of letter and papers on the "table of doom" as I needed someone to keep me company and make sure I got these mundane tasks finished. The friends who invited us to spend Christmas Eve with them and helped me pack up the house when we left, practical stuff. The friends who checked on me and one who flew out from the UK to simply be with me for a week while I was going through my husband's things before we moved.' Hayley

Epilogue

Reassurances from the future

When I was writing this book what struck me was the underlying theme of worry. Worry about doing it right. Worry for the future. Worry about how things would turn out. I think most parents feel this way at one time or other, but it can be exacerbated as a single parent. When you're making decisions alone, the weight can feel heavy. It can feel like there's more of a spotlight on you, waiting for things to go wrong so people can point the 'single parent' finger.

We can't predict the future but what I realised we could do was listen to the voices of adults who had a single parent growing up. Let's face it, although they can be lovely, teenagers do have a bit of a habit sometimes of thinking everything is so unfair, so I thought I'd skip asking them and go instead to those people who had had time to reflect and look back on their experience of being brought up by a single parent. I asked them two questions and here are some of their very reassuring words.

Why Single Parents Matter

1. What did your single parent do well that has stuck with you until today?

'My mum wasn't afraid to show emotion in front of me. She was honest about when she was finding things hard. This taught me a lot. It helped me be honest.' Tori H, 31

'My mum just always kept things "normal". There was never any drama or fuss, no matter what was going on with my parents, we still went to school, we still ate dinner, and we still saw our dad without any negativity. It's only now that I have my own kids that I realise how complicated and painful that must have been at the time.' Sarah, 33

'My Mum was always there for me. Talking to me, making time for me and supporting me with my emotions. She thought very carefully about how to talk to me about death, and was honest with me in an age-appropriate way (I was four when my Dad died). She made sure I was included in discussions, funeral planning and grave visits as she knew that it was important for me to be a part of that and not feel excluded. This all helped me to understand and process what was happening and to feel like my loss was valid and respected too. I still remember the feeling of being included in the collective grief and I am so grateful to have experienced this and not have it brushed away.' Emmie, 35

'As someone who ended up being a single parent to a six-week old baby until she was four years old, my mother was a beacon of hope for me when I was living back at home after leaving my daughter's dad. I've always looked at how far my mum came as a single parent and knew that it was only a limitation put on me by others, and

How to support a single parent

that I could do anything I wanted to. She always used to tell me "You'll do it because you have no choice" and it's always pushed me through hard times.' Kasey, 29

'Creating family experiences even on a tight budget like when we grew flowers and letting me have a vegetable patch. Days out to the local park even in the rain and dinner picnics on the living room floor.' Grace Munro, 33

'Mum never bad-mouthed dad and vice versa and they made sure grandparents did the same. While it was a scary time I never felt anything but love for my family and it has helped me through times of change as I've grown older knowing I have a secure base.' Lucy-Jayne Costello, 39

'I was five and don't remember the separation but I do remember the heartache of dad not showing up. But mum never talked bad about him. She gave me and my brother so much love and support during that time.' Ffion Austin, 35

'My mum validated my feelings of hurt, anger and resentment. And encouraged me to let it go. She never pressured me to have a relationship with my now-estranged dad. She let me decide as an independently thinking teen. She never really let us feel her hurt though. She kept her pain and tears from us and carried on with an unwavering energy and enthusiasm for being kind, hardworking and hopeful in life.' Jenna, 38

'My mum put focus on me, looking far ahead into my future and dreaming about the things that I could do that

she didn't have the opportunity to do. Every year, without fail, I buy a father's day card and give it to my mum. It's a little tradition that I've built and I believe it means more to her than mother's day.' Laura McGuire, 34

'I was too young to remember and don't feel I missed out on having my dad around. But one thing my mum did was surround me with positive father figures such as my uncle and grandad and I always had a lovely relationship with them. Also my mum never hid anything from me and was always honest with me while protecting me at the same time. Growing up, I always felt loved and secure.' Trudi, 51

2. What would you say if you could go back in time and reassure your single parent?

'You are enough, you are everything I need.' Anne-Marie, 43

'You are a superhero to raise a human on your own. Don't ever disregard your strengths. Raising a child takes a village. But doing it alone makes this even more important.' Triumphs and tribulations of solo parenting, 21

'You did your best. I always felt loved, supported and encouraged. You had the perfect balance of keeping a tight rein but freedom to explore too. You should be proud.' Michelle, 38

'Mum, it still amazes me that you were only fourteen when I was born. It will take time but I will come to love how different our family was, how unconventional and how unfailingly supportive and present you were.' Emmy, 32

How to support a single parent

'Seeing you handle everything so expertly on your own taught me how to be strong, independent and resilient by osmosis. This was the best kind of role model I could have ever had – so good, in fact, that I have now decided to become a single parent by donor conception because you have shown me how possible single parenthood is!' Ali, 41

'You were amazing and still are amazing. Your strength is still a wonder to me and I will always be grateful for the sacrifices you made. You are a wonderful human and amazing mum! I never felt blamed. I always knew I was loved. A million thank yous for being you!' Michaela, 34

'When times were uncertain, you remained our certainty. Our unconditional loving constant'. Shpleckii, 30

'You're not going to be able to do everything, and that's ok. Just being there for things meant the world to me.' George, 31

'You're doing an amazing job raising two daughters on your own, you don't need to sacrifice so much for their happiness, we're happiest when we're with you.' Sharon, 36

'Thank you for challenging gender norms as a single mum. You inadvertently taught me that women can do anything. From a young age you taught me I could do whatever I wanted through your own actions. Parenting is the hardest job in the world, and to tackle it alone (through choice or otherwise) deserves significant praise and recognition.' Daisy, 35

'Dear Mum, we made it, you raised three children by

> *yourself who have all succeeded in life with beautiful families, degrees and jobs of their own now, I'm sure there were times when you didn't think you could get through or if you felt you let us down as we didn't have a present father but you were all we needed, the love we had from you consistently through the years is what has made us into the great adults we are now. I didn't quite understand how much you went through until I became a mother myself, I truly do not know how you did it throughout the years. There were bumps in the road, you didn't give up though. You kept on pushing through, our relationship has never been better, and I thank you so much for bringing me into this world even though I know at times you thought you might have made a mistake after our father leaving you to do it all by yourself. You are my hero, my inspiration and I will forever love you and care for you.'* Ellen, 26

I now appear to have something in my eye, so we'll come to a close. Good luck, you've got this.

Resources

Useful organisations

Gingerbread: A wealth of support and information for single parents including online chat www.gingerbread.org.uk or 0808 802 0925

Family Lives: Live chat, email and phone support for families www.familylives.org.uk or 0808 800 2222

Citizens Advice has information on separation www.citizensadvice.org.uk/family/how-to-separate1/deciding-what-to-do-when-you-separate

Relate can offer support on family counselling and supporting your child www.relate.org.uk

The NSPCC has lots of information about divorce and separation www.nspcc.org.uk/keeping-children-safe/support-for-parents/separation-and-divorce

Children and Family Court Advisory and Support Service (CAFCASS) for legal information about separation www.cafcass.gov.uk/about-cafcass

Winston's Wish: Support for bereavement for children, teenagers and young adults www.winstonswish.org

Child Bereavement UK www.childbereavementuk.org/supporting-bereaved-children-and-young-people

MIND offer mental health support www.mind.org.uk

Barnardo's offer adoption support www.barnardos.org.uk/adopt/adoption-support

Adoption UK also supports children and teens who have been adopted, and the parents who adopt them www.adoptionuk.org

Solo Mothers by Choice is a US group but has a great UK Facebook page community www.facebook.com/groups/473506363502195. Another social media page

dedicated to single mothering by choice is
@noneedforprincecharming

Support lines for children
CAFCASS **www.cafcass.gov.uk/young-people** or 08081753333
Childline **www.childline.org.uk** or 0800 1111
Young Minds supporting child and teenage mental health **www.youngminds.org.uk**

References

2: Where did stereotypes about single parenting come from?

1. Thane, P. & Evans, T. (2012) *Sinners? Scroungers? Saints?: Unmarried Motherhood in Twentieth-Century England.* OUP.
2. https://www.gingerbread.org.uk/your-community/stories/single-parent-history-the-foundling-hospital/
3. https://foundlingmuseum.org.uk/our-story/history/
4. https://www.nationalarchives.gov.uk/education/resources/1834-poor-law/#:~:text=The%20new%20Poor%20Law%20ensured,shared%20this%20point%20of%20view.
5. https://api.parliament.uk/historic-hansard/commons/1925/apr/28/widows-and-old-age-pensions
6. https://www.independent.co.uk/news/uk/this-britain/sin-and-the-single-mother-the-history-of-lone-parenthood-7782370.html
7. https://www.salvationarmy.org.uk/mother-and-baby-homes
8. https://hansard.parliament.uk/commons/1993-07-20/debates/9f19e15c-1951-4b86-8162-1de2d1327bc3/SocialSecurityAndTheWelfareState
9. https://api.parliament.uk/historic-hansard/commons/1993/jul/05/single-mothers
10. https://www.bsa.natcen.ac.uk/latest-report/british-social-attitudes-30/spending-and-welfare/welfare-benefits.aspx

3: Is there any evidence that children from single parent families have worse outcomes?

1. Bernardi, L. et al (2018). Changing lone parents, changing life courses. *Lone parenthood in the life course*, 1-26.
2. Pearce, A. et al (2013). The role of poverty in explaining health variations in 7-year-old children from different family structures: findings from the UK Millennium Cohort Study. *JECH*, 67(2), 181-189.
3. Pong, S. et al. (2003). Family policies and children's school achievement in single-versus two-parent families. *Journal of marriage and family*, 65(3), 681-699.
4. Alami, A. et al (2014). Adolescents' self-esteem in Chan, R. et al (1998). Psychosocial adjustment among children conceived via donor insemination by lesbian and heterosexual mothers. *Child

Development, 69,443–457

5. Murray, C., & Golombok, S. (2005a). Going it alone: Solo mothers and their infants conceived by donor insemination. *American Journal of Orthopsychiatry*, 75,242–253
6. Murray, C., & Golombok, S. (2005b). Solo mothers and their donor insemination infants: Follow-up at age 2 years. *Human Reproduction*,20,1655–1660
7. Golombok S. et al (2016) Single mothers by choice: Mother–child relationships and children's psychological adjustment. *Journal of Family Psychology*, 30(4):409.
8. Agnafors S. et al (2019) Mental health in young mothers, single mothers and their children. *BMC psychiatry*, 9(1):1-7.
9. Meltzer, H. et al (2003). Mental health of children and adolescents in Great Britain. *International review of Psychiatry*, 15 (1-2), 185-187.
10. Burns C., Cook K., Mavoa H. Role of expendable income and price in food choice by low income families. Appetite. 2013 Dec 1;71:209-17.
11. McKenzie H.J., McKay F.H. Food as a discretionary item: the impact of welfare payment changes on low-income single mother's food choices and strategies. *Journal of Poverty and Social Justice*. 2017 Feb 27;25(1):35-48.
12. Lutenbacher, M. (2000). Perceptions of health status and the relationship with abuse history and mental health in low-income single mothers. *Journal of Family Nursing*, 6(4), 320-340.
13. Wuest, J. et al. (2003). Intrusion: The central problem for family health promotion among children and single mothers after leaving an abusive partner. *Qualitative Health Research*, 13 (5), 597-622.
14. Bowman, D., & Wickramasinghe, S. (2020). Trampolines not traps: enabling economic security for single mothers and their children.
15. Collings, S. et al (2014). Gender differences in the mental health of single parents: New Zealand evidence from a household panel survey. *SPPE*, *49*, 811-821.
16. Jones, C. et al (2022). Solo fathers and mothers: An exploration of well-being, social support and social approval. *IJERPH*, *19*(15), 9236.

6: Dealing with finances

1. Skinner, C. and Main, G. (2013), 'The contribution of child

maintenance payments to the income packages of lone mothers', *Journal of Poverty and Social Justice*, 21: 1, 47–60.
2. Grall, T. (2016), Custodial Mothers and Fathers and their Child Support: 2013. Washington, DC: U.S Census Bureau
3. Cook, K. et al (2015), 'The contribution of child support payments to the income packages of lone mothers in Australia', Presentation at ESRC International Research Seminar Series, Child Maintenance: International Perspectives & Policy Challenges, London, July 2015
4. Cook, K., Goodall, Z., Mclaren, J. and Edwards, T. (2019) *Debts and Disappointment: Mothers' Experiences of the Child Support System*, Melbourne: Swinburne University of Technology. https://researchbank.swinburne.edu.au/file/8e625e6a-3ae4-40d1-a426-474bba91d620/1/2019-cook-debts_and_disappointment.pdf
5. Griffith, A.K. (2022). Parental burnout and child maltreatment during the COVID-19 pandemic. *Journal of family violence*, 37(5), 725-731.
6. Sharp-Jeffs, N. (2021) Understanding the economics of abuse: an assessment of the economic abuse definition within the Domestic Abuse Bill, *Journal of Gender-Based Violence*, 5(1): 163–73.
7. Adams, A. et al (2008) Development of the scale of economic Abuse, *Violence Against Women*, 14: 562–88
8. Toews, M.L. and Bermea, A.M. (2017) 'I was naïve in thinking, "I divorced this man, he is out of my life"': a qualitative exploration of post-separation power and control tactics experienced by women, *Journal of Interpersonal Violence*, 32(14): 2166–89
9. McKenzie H.J., McKay F.H. Food as a discretionary item: the impact of welfare payment changes on low-income single mother's food choices. *Journal of Poverty and Social Justice*. 2017 27;25(1):35-48.

8: Thriving (and healing) as a single parent

1. www.oxfordclinicalpsych.com/page/winnicott-radio-bbc
2. Brown, B. *Daring Greatly: How the Courage to Be Vulnerable Transforms the Way We Live, Love, Parent, and Lead*. 2018. Penguin.
3. Obama, M. (2022) *The Light We Carry: Overcoming in Uncertain Times*. Penguin.
4. Wendelboe-Nelson C et al. A scoping review mapping research on green space and associated mental health benefits. *IJERPH*. 2019 Jan;16(12):2081.

5. Huttunen P. et al (2004) Winter swimming improves general well-being. *International Journal of Circumpolar Health*. 1;63(2):140-4.
6. Song H et al. Effect of self-administered foot reflexology for symptom management in healthy persons: systematic review & meta-analysis. *Complementary Therapies in Medicine*. 2015 1:79-89.
7. Hilton L et al. Meditation for posttraumatic stress: Systematic review and meta-analysis. *Psychological Trauma: Theory, Research, Practice, and Policy*. 2017 Jul;9(4):453.
8. Pascoe M. et al, (2017) Mindfulness mediates the physiological markers of stress: systematic review and meta-analysis. *Journal of Psychiatric Research*, 1;95:156-78.
9. Van Lith T. Art therapy in mental health. *The Arts in Psychotherapy*, 2016, 47, 9-22.

Index

absent co-parents 75, 77–8
'absent father' stereotype 34
absolute versus relative risk 45, 46
abusive relationships
    co-parenting 75, 79, 81
    effect on mental health 50–1, 125–6
    financial abuse 94–5
accepting help that is offered 132–4
Action for Children 68
additional needs, children with 65, 103
adoption 20, 22, 30, 47, 61, 86, 134
adult company (lack of) 22
advice for supporters of single parents 139–42
All Party Parliamentary Groups 97
alternate week arrangements 64
anger 53, 54, 55, 62, 71, 117
anxiety 48, 51, 53, 54, 55, 95, 123, 125
asking for help 133–4
asthma 46
attachment 54, 70, 112
autonomy 40, 101, 102, 104

babies/toddlers
    adjusting arrangements over time 66
    co-parenting 69–71
    degree of shared care 64
babysitters 135
balancing children and a new partner 103–4
balancing work/life/children 21, 53, 83
battles, picking your 76
behavioural outcomes 48
benefits 37, 82, 84–6, 105
bereavement 21, 47, 53, 54, 98, 125
    support for 56
Bereavement Support Benefit 85–6

best interests of child at heart of decisions 63, 73, 77–8
birthdays 69
blame 30, 34, 43, 58
blended families 98, 101–15
breaches of court arrangements 74
break, getting a 26–7, 135
breastfed infants 64, 69–71
Brown, Brené 120–1

CAFCASS 58–9, 67, 73, 77, 81
calming your system 121–3
child arrangement orders 73–4
child benefit 84–5
child contact centres 71–2
child maintenance payments 83, 87–95
Child Maintenance Service (CMS) 89, 92–3, 94, 96
Child Support Agency 94
childcare circles 134–5
childcare costs 83–4, 87, 90
choice, single parenthood by 20, 30, 47–8, 53, 86
choosing your battles 76
Citizen's Advice 72, 85
clothing, between houses 67
Collect and Pay service 89, 93
comfort items 67
communication between co-parents 66–7, 72–3, 74–7
conflict, parental 48 *see also* abusive relationships
connection with children 19–20
contact with other parent *see also* co-parenting
    as a 'break' from single parenting 26–9
    concerns over ability of other parent to properly care for children 27, 50, 71–2
    degree of shared care 63–7

as ongoing abuse 50–1
  pressures on single parents to ensure 51
control 28–9, 76, 81, 95
co-parenting 62–81
  adjusting arrangements over time 66
  babies/toddlers 69–71
  concerns over ability of other parent to properly care for children 27, 50, 71–2
  coping when children are with their other parent 26–30
  degree of shared care 63–7
  difficult co-parenting relationships 72–4
  equally-shared care 64
  grief at lack of co-parent at all 62
  improvement in relationship between exes 9–10
  keeping a friendly and united appearance 59
  shared routines and rules 59, 66–7
  when co-parent is difficult 50
counter-dependency 133
court orders 28, 50–1, 70, 72–4, 88
Covid-19 94
creativity 124

definition of single parent 8–11
depression 49–51, 95, 123, 125
diaries 66, 76
difficulties of single parenting 21–31
disabilities, children with 65, 103
'Disney Dad' 27, 51, 137
Domestic Abuse Act (2021) 95

economic abuse *see* financial abuse
educational outcomes 47, 48
emotional support 140, 142
emotions 21, 55–7, 68, 79–80, 113, 121
Entitled To 85, 87
equally-shared care 64

every other weekend 26
exercise 122
ex-partners *see also* co-parenting; other parent
  communication with 74–7
  difficult co-parenting relationships 72–4
extended family 60

Family Mediation Council 73
father-child relationship 51
'feeling like a' single parent 10, 24
feelings, talking about 55–6, 68, 79
finances 82–97 *see also* benefits
  financial support (from government) 82–7
  new relationships 106
  poverty 43, 47, 49–50, 82
  refusal to pay child maintenance 50, 78, 92–7
  related to amount of care 28, 92–5
  surviving on one income 82–3
  welfare state 37–8, 39–40
financial abuse 75, 94–5
food and nutrition 50
food banks 85
'for the sake of the children,' staying together 48
foundlings 36
freedom 18–20, 101–2
Freedom Programme 126
friends, support from 119–21, 139–42
friendships, children's 65, 68, 139
fun with your child 137
future, worrying about the 21, 53, 143

gaslighting 51
Gilbert, Paul 127
Gingerbread 41, 54, 81
Godfrey-Isaacs, Laura 124
'good enough' parenting 54, 118, 128
grandparents 60

Index

grief 56, 62, 71, 117 *see also* bereavement
grocery shopping 131–2
grounding techniques 123
guardians, setting up 136
guilt 23, 71, 95, 135
gut instinct, following 61

handovers 76
happy memories, supporting 60–1
headlines and stereotypes 32–41
health and wellbeing outcomes (children) 46
Healthy Start scheme 85
help, asking for 133–4
history of single motherhood 35–9
holiday childcare 83–4
homes, having two 67
housing 65, 67, 107–8

'I don't know how you do it' 30–1
income, reduced 82 *see also* finances; poverty
inner critic, ignoring 126–9
interests of child at heart of decisions 63, 73, 77–8
Ireland 38–9
IVF 30, 40, 48, 54, 86

Jackson, Glenda 40
juggling 21, 53, 83

La Leche League 71
lazy/undeserving tropes 34, 39–41
legal aid 73
legalities 135–6
life insurance 136
Lilley, Peter 40
listening 55–6
loneliness 49
longitudinal studies 46
loved, reassuring children they are 54–5, 79
low-paid jobs 84

maintenance payments 83, 87–95
male single parents 35
Maternal Journal 124
McGowan, Samantha 124
mediation 63, 72–3
meditation 123
Men's Advice 72
mental health
　difficult co-parenting relationships 75
　exercise and time outdoors 122–3
　financial abuse 95
　negative effects on maternal mental health 43, 48, 49–51
　paternal mental health 49, 51
　poverty 49–50
　professional support/therapy 124–9
　teenage 44
　your right to receive support for 116
Millennium Cohort study 46
mindfulness 123
misogyny 34
Money Saving Expert 85
mother-and-baby homes 38–9
Motherland 129

National Association of Child Contact Centres (NACCC) 71–2
neutral ground 76
new relationships 9, 98–115
　challenges 101–7
　effect of ex's new relationships on child maintenance 91–2
　new partner is not the same as a co-parent 25
　parenting role of new partner 106, 109
　positives 98–101
　timing of introducing to children 110
NSPCC 73–4, 81, 108

157

Obama, Michelle 121
obesity 46
'one day at a time' 117–18
other parent *see also* contact with other parent; co-parenting
  effect of your own new relationship on 114–15
  keeping a friendly and united appearance with 59, 67–8
  parents staying in the other parent's house 70
  supporting your child through their time away from you 67–8
  supporting your child when their other parent treats them badly 78–81
  talking to children about 57–8, 76
  when they don't want contact 77–8
'othering' 35
outcomes for children of single parents 42–51
outdoors, time 123
overnights, building up to 70
overwhelm 23
oxygen mask analogy 116–17

parenting plans 66
paternal mental health 49, 51
Paton, Maureen 38
patterns of shared care 64
photos and memories 60–1
Pickett, Emma 71
Poor Laws 37
'popping out,' impossibility of 131
positive and silver linings 18–20
poverty 43, 47, 49–50, 82
pregnancy-outside-marriage, history of 36, 37
pride in managing alone 21
professional support/therapy 56, 124–9

questions, children's 54

reasons for separation, telling children about 57–8
refusal to pay child maintenance 50, 78, 92–7
refusal to see child (parent) 77–8
refusal to see other parent (child) 74, 80, 81
regret 21
Relate 56
religion 36, 40
responsibility, holding all the 24–5, 29
Riddick, Graham 40
'rights of the father' 75
'rights' to contact with children 51, 81
risk, absolute versus relative 45, 46
routines 59, 66–7, 110, 128, 138

safe living/meeting spaces 71–2
safety concerns 71–2, 77, 80–1
Salvation Army homes 38
schools
  considering in shared-care arrangements 64–5
  informing 56
secure, helping children feel 54–5
self-compassion 127
self-criticism 126–9
self-massage 123
separation anxiety 68
shame 36, 37–8, 40, 53, 127
shared diaries 66
shopping practicalities 131–2
sibling and step-sibling relationships 111–12, 113–14
sickness (children's) 84
'single mother' stereotypes 33–5
single motherhood, history of 35–9
Single Parents Rights 41, 97
skipping meals 50

Index

social attitudes to single parents 32–41, 120
social services 71
stability for children 64
stalking 50
staying in the other parent's house 70
step-children 104, 108 *see also* blended families
stereotypes 32–41
stress 76, 122
student loans 92
super parent, no requirement to be a 44
support for yourself
    during children's contact with other parent 68–9
    practical tips 130–8
    professional support/therapy 56, 124–9
    support networks 56, 76–7, 119–21, 132–4
    support organisations 136–7, 149–50
    thriving and healing 116–29
    when you need additional support 124–9
supporting a single parent (advice for supporters) 139–42
supporting children through change 52–61

tax-free childcare scheme 87
teenagers 66, 79–80, 110, 113
Thatcher, Margaret 40
therapy/professional support 56
threatening behaviours 72
time for yourself 26–7, 137–8, 140
transitions
    children's ability to cope with 65, 67
    handovers 76
    rituals 69
trauma 39, 68–9
Trent, Marianne 126–9
tribe, finding your 128–9, 134
Trussell Trust 85
truth, telling children the 57–8

undeserving single mother tropes 34, 39–41
Universal Credit 82, 87, 92
unreliability on the other parent's part 78–9

weaning 71
welfare state 37, 40
Widowed Parent's Allowance 86
wills 135–6
Winnicott, Donald 118
wishes of children 73–4
withholding access to a child 73
Women's Aid 72
workhouses 36–7
working
    flexibility 84
    juggling work and childcare 83–4
    and maintenance payments 92–5
    supporting single parents' access to 47
    working patterns and shared-care arrangements 65
World Health Organization 69
'worry boxes' 68
written communication, importance of 75

yoga breathing 123
younger single parents, stereotypes of 34

*Available from Pinter & Martin
in the Why it Matters series*

1. *Why Your Baby's Sleep Matters* Sarah Ockwell-Smith
2. *Why Hypnobirthing Matters* Katrina Berry
3. *Why Doulas Matter* Maddie McMahon
4. *Why Postnatal Depression Matters* Mia Scotland
5. *Why Babywearing Matters* Rosie Knowles
6. *Why the Politics of Breastfeeding Matter* Gabrielle Palmer
7. *Why Breastfeeding Matters* Charlotte Young
8. *Why Starting Solids Matters* Amy Brown
9. *Why Human Rights in Childbirth Matter* Rebecca Schiller
10. *Why Mothers' Medication Matters* Wendy Jones
11. *Why Home Birth Matters* Natalie Meddings
12. *Why Caesarean Matters* Clare Goggin
13. *Why Mothering Matters* Maddie McMahon
14. *Why Induction Matters* Rachel Reed
15. *Why Birth Trauma Matters* Emma Svanberg
16. *Why Oxytocin Matters* Kerstin Uvnäs Moberg
17. *Why Breastfeeding Grief and Trauma Matter* Amy Brown
18. *Why Postnatal Recovery Matters* Sophie Messager
19. *Why Pregnancy and Postnatal Exercise Matter* Rehana Jawadwala
20. *Why Baby Loss Matters* Kay King
21. *Why Infant Reflux Matters* Carol Smyth
22. *Why Tongue-tie Matters* Sarah Oakley
23. *Why Formula Feeding Matters* Shel Banks
24. *Why Grandmothers Matter* Naomi Stadlen
25. *Why Mixed Feeding Matters* Karen Hall
26. *Why Single Parents Matter* Amy Brown
27. *Why Childhood Illness Matters* Lyndsey Hookway

Series editor: Susan Last

pinterandmartin.com